LEICA D-LUX (TYP 109) USER GUIDE

The Photographer's Manual to Get the Best from the 4/3-Inch Sensor and Bright f/1.7-2.8 Lens Compact Camera

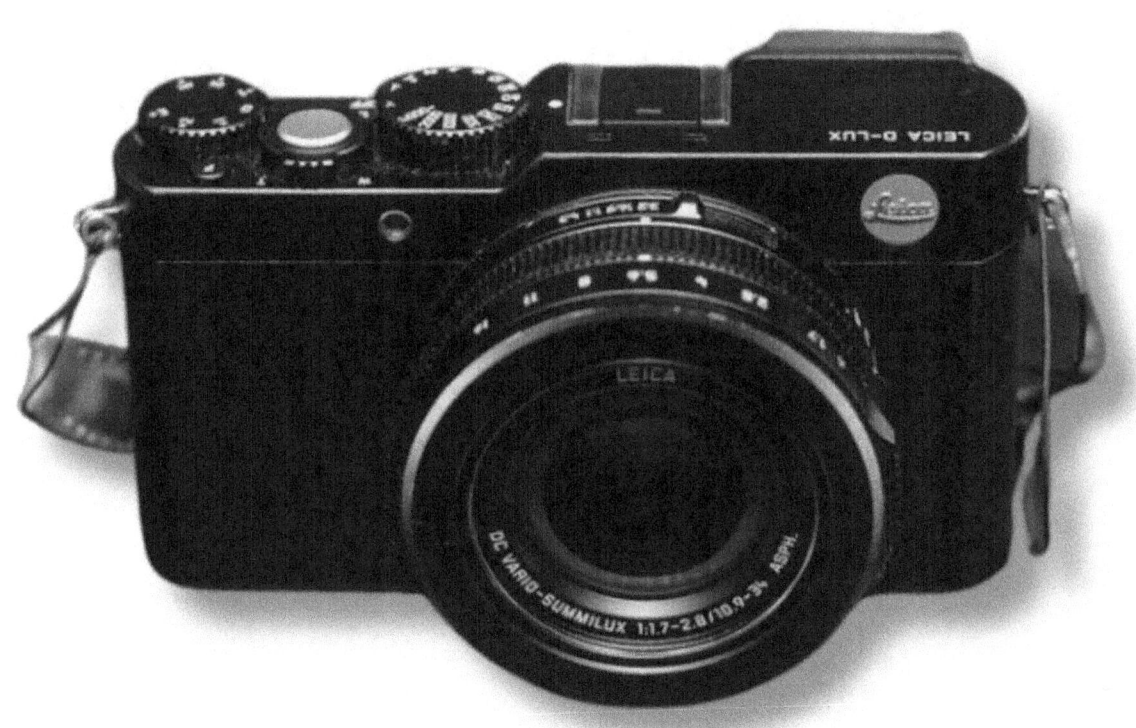

ROBERT M. OVERTON

Copyright © 2024 Robert M. Overton

Unauthorized reproduction, distribution, or transmission of any part of this publication in any form or by any means, including photocopying, recording, or other electronic or mechanical methods, without the prior written permission of the publisher, is prohibited.

Brief quotations may be used in critical reviews and other non-commercial uses permitted by copyright law, provided proper attribution is given.

TABLE OF CONTENTS

DISCLAIMER	6
CHAPTER ONE	8
INTRODUCTION	8
Overview of Leica D-Lux (Typ 109)	8
What's in the Box	10
CHAPTER TWO	12
CAMERA OVERVIEW	12
Front View Layout	12
Top View Layout	17
Buttons and Controls	18
CHAPTER THREE	21
GETTING STARTED	21
Charging the Battery	21
Inserting the Battery and Memory Card	22
Powering On/Off	23
Setting Up Date and Time	24
Setting the Language	27
CHAPTER FOUR	30
BASIC OPERATION	30
Shutter Release Button	33
Zooming	34
Capturing Images	36
Playback Mode	39
CHAPTER FIVE	44
ADVANCED SHOOTING MODES	44
Aperture Priority Mode (A)	44
Shutter Priority Mode (S)	47
Manual Mode (M)	50
Program Mode (P)	52
Scene Modes (SCN)	54
Creative Modes	56
CHAPTER SIX	60
CAMERA OVERVIEW	60

    Autofocus (AF) Settings 60

    Exposure Compensation 63

    ISO Sensitivity 64

    Metering Modes 66

CHAPTER SEVEN 70

WHITE BALANCE AND COLOUR SETTINGS 70

    Auto White Balance 70

    Preset White Balance Options 71

    Custom White Balance 72

    Picture Styles 74

CHAPTER EIGHT 76

VIDEO RECORDING 76

    Video Resolution and Frame Rates 76

    Recording Videos 78

    Audio Settings 80

    Playback of Recorded Videos 81

CHAPTER NINE 84

FLASH PHOTOGRAPHY 84

    Built-in Flash Settings 84

    Flash Modes 86

    External Flash Compatibility 88

CHAPTER TEN 90

WIFI AND CONNECTIVITY 90

    Enabling Wi-Fi 90

    Connecting to Smart Devices 91

    Using the Leica Image Shuttle App 93

    Transferring Photos to a Computer 95

CHAPTER ELEVEN 98

ACCESSORIES AND COMPATIBILITY 98

    Compatible Lenses and Accessories 98

    Using Tripods and Other Supports 99

    Optional External Microphones 101

CHAPTER TWELVE 104

MAINTEMNANCE AND CARE 104

    Cleaning the Camera and Lens 104

- Storing the Camera 105
- Updating Firmware 107
- Troubleshooting Common Issues 108

CHAPTER THIRTEEN 110

- TECHNICAL SPECIFICATION 110
- Lens Specifications 111
- Battery Life and Usage 112

DISCLAIMER

The contents of this book are provided for informational and entertainment purposes only. The author and publisher do not make any representations or warranties regarding the accuracy, applicability, completeness, or suitability of the contents for any purpose.

The information in this book is based on the author's personal experiences, research, and opinions, and should not be considered a substitute for professional advice. Readers are advised to consult appropriate professionals regarding their specific situations.

The author and publisher are not liable for any loss, injury, or damage allegedly arising from the information or suggestions in this book. Any reliance on such information is at the reader's own risk.

The inclusion of third-party resources, websites, or references does not imply endorsement or responsibility for their content or services.

Readers are encouraged to use their own discretion and judgment when applying the information or recommendations in this book to their own lives.

All rights reserved. No part of this book may be reproduced, distributed, or transmitted in any form or by any means without the prior written permission of the publisher, except for brief quotations in critical reviews and certain other non-commercial uses permitted by copyright law.

Thank you for reading and understanding this disclaimer.

CHAPTER ONE
INTRODUCTION

Overview of Leica D-Lux (Typ 109)

The **Leica D-Lux (Typ 109)** is a compact, high-performance camera known for its sophisticated design, exceptional image quality, and portability. It combines advanced technology with a simple interface, making it a versatile tool for both amateur photographers and seasoned professionals. Here are some key highlights of the camera:

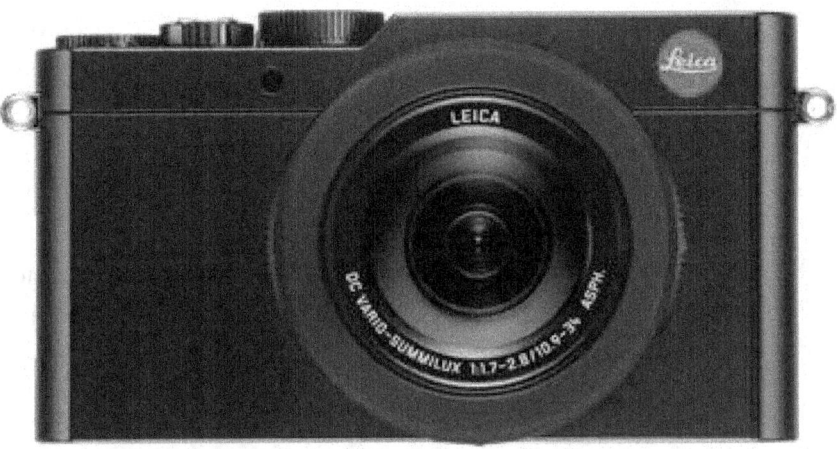

Key Features:

1. **Micro Four Thirds Sensor**
   - The D-Lux features a large 12.8 MP Micro Four Thirds sensor, which is significantly larger than most sensors found in compact cameras. This sensor size allows for better light capture, resulting in high-quality images with excellent detail and clarity, even in low-light situations.

2. **Leica DC Vario-Summilux 24-75mm f/1.7-2.8 Lens**
   - The fast Leica Vario-Summilux lens offers a versatile zoom range, covering wide-angle to short telephoto focal lengths. Its bright aperture allows for creative depth-of-field effects and excellent performance in low-light environments.

3. **4K Video Recording**
   - The D-Lux is capable of recording 4K UHD video at 30 fps. This high resolution provides sharp, detailed footage, and users can also extract high-quality still images from their 4K videos.

4. **Built-in Wi-Fi with NFC**
   - Integrated Wi-Fi and Near Field Communication (NFC) enable users to connect the camera to a smartphone or tablet easily. This allows for wireless image sharing, remote control shooting, and access to the Leica Image Shuttle app.

5. **High-Resolution Electronic Viewfinder (EVF)**
   - The camera includes a 2.76 million-dot electronic viewfinder that delivers a clear and sharp view of the scene, helping users frame shots with precision.

6. **Compact and Stylish Design**
   - The D-Lux is designed to be compact and lightweight, making it highly portable for everyday photography and travel. Its sleek design and classic Leica aesthetic appeal to photographers who value both performance and style.

7. **Fast Autofocus and Manual Control**
   - With fast autofocus capabilities, the D-Lux ensures that subjects are captured with speed and accuracy. The camera also supports full manual control, providing flexibility for photographers who want to adjust settings such as aperture, shutter speed, and ISO manually.

8. **Multiple Exposure and Focus Modes**
   - The camera offers a variety of exposure and focus modes, including Program (P), Aperture Priority (A), Shutter Priority (S), and Manual (M), giving users creative control over their photography.

9. **Built-in Flash and Hot Shoe**
   - The D-Lux includes a pop-up flash for quick lighting needs and a hot shoe for attaching external flashes or other accessories.

Design and Usability

The D-Lux 8 has undergone a design overhaul compared to the D-Lux 7, aligning more closely with Leica's aesthetic and user interface. It features a simplified menu system and a customizable command dial, enhancing user experience. The camera lacks a built-in flash but includes a small external flash unit that connects via the hot shoe.

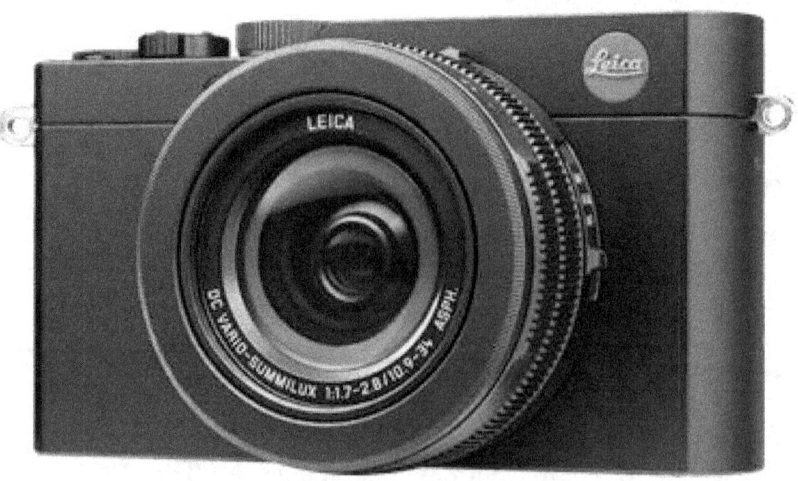

Performance

While the D-Lux 8 excels in good lighting conditions, its low-light performance has been criticized. The camera's high ISO capabilities are deemed subpar, with aggressive noise reduction affecting image quality in darker settings. However, under optimal conditions, it delivers sharp images with vibrant colours.

Reception

The D-Lux 8 has been received with mixed reviews. Critics appreciate the aesthetic improvements and simplified controls but note that it does not significantly enhance image quality over the D-Lux 7. The price point of approximately $1,595 positions it as a premium compact camera, competing with models like the Fujifilm X100VI, which some reviewers regard as superior in terms of overall performance.

Ideal for:

- Street photography, travel, and everyday shooting due to its compact size and wide range of focal lengths.
- Low-light photography with its fast lens and large sensor.
- Videography with its 4K video recording capabilities.

In summary, the Leica D-Lux 8 is a stylish and compact camera ideal for enthusiasts looking for a blend of classic design and modern features, though it may not meet the expectations of those seeking exceptional low-light performance.

What's in the Box

When purchasing the **Leica D-Lux (Typ 109)**, the following items are typically included in the box:

1. **Leica D-Lux (Typ 109) Camera Body**
   - The main compact camera body, featuring a built-in lens.

2. **Leica DC Vario-Summilux 24-75mm f/1.7-2.8 Lens**
   - The fixed, built-in zoom lens with a versatile focal range and bright aperture.

3. **Lens Cap**
   - A protective cap for covering the front of the lens when not in use.

4. **Hot Shoe Cover**
   - A small cover to protect the camera's hot shoe mount when not in use.

5. **Battery (BP-DC15)**
   - A rechargeable lithium-ion battery designed specifically for the D-Lux (Typ 109).

6. **Battery Charger (BC-DC15)**
    - The charger for recharging the included battery.

7. **USB Cable**
    - For connecting the camera to a computer or other devices for data transfer.

8. **Carrying Strap**
    - A neck or wrist strap to safely carry the camera.

9. **Lens Hood**
    - An accessory to reduce lens flare and protect the lens from stray light.

10. **Flash Unit**
    - A compact, attachable external flash for better control over lighting in low-light conditions.

11. **Software License for Adobe Photoshop Lightroom**
    - A download license for the popular photo editing software, which allows users to manage and edit their photos.

12. **Printed Quick Start Guide**
    - A basic manual that introduces the camera's features and guides you through initial setup and operation.

13. **Warranty Card**
    - The official warranty document for product registration and service.

These accessories and components are designed to help you get started with your Leica D-Lux (Typ 109) right out of the box.

CHAPTER TWO
CAMERA OVERVIEW

Front View Layout

The front view of the **Leica D-Lux (Typ 109)** camera includes several key elements that provide functionality and aesthetic appeal. Here's a breakdown of the front view layout:

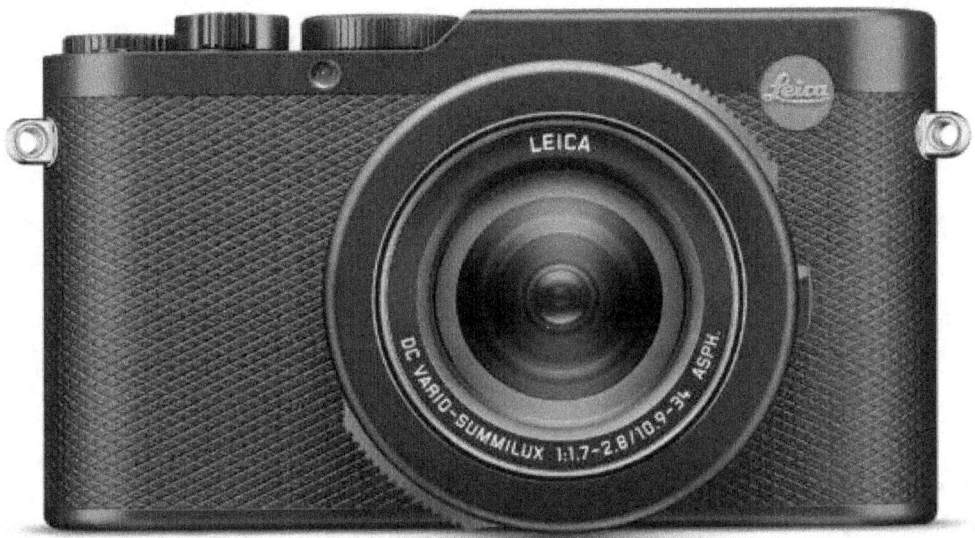

1. **Leica DC Vario-Summilux 24-75mm f/1.7-2.8 Lens**

   o The fixed zoom lens dominates the front of the camera, featuring a versatile focal range and bright aperture for enhanced image quality.

2. **Lens Control Ring**

   o A manual ring around the lens allows for easy adjustment of settings such as zoom or focus, providing a tactile interface for creative control.

3. **Built-in Microphone**

   o Small openings located near the lens capture sound during video recording. The built-in microphone is stereo, providing good audio quality for videos.

4. **Lens Cap (Attached)**

   o The lens cap protects the lens from dust and scratches when not in use.

5. **AF Assist Lamp**

   o Located near the lens, the autofocus (AF) assist lamp helps improve focusing performance in low-light conditions by illuminating the subject briefly.

6. **Flash Pop-Up Button**

   o Positioned near the top of the camera, this button activates the built-in flash to pop up for use in low-light settings.

7. **Leica Logo**
   - The iconic red Leica logo is displayed prominently on the front, signifying the camera's heritage and quality craftsmanship.

8. **Grip Area**
   - The textured grip on the right side provides a comfortable and secure hold while shooting.

9. **Focus Mode Selector**
   - Located on the side of the lens barrel, this switch allows the user to toggle between autofocus (AF) and manual focus (MF) modes. This quick access helps in adjusting the focus based on the shooting situation, whether you prefer manual control or automatic focusing.

10. **Zoom Ring**
    - Alongside the control ring, the zoom ring encircling the lens allows for smooth, precise adjustments of focal length. This feature is particularly useful when framing shots and offers tactile feedback for greater control over zooming in and out.

11. **Shutter Release Button**
    - Although more prominent in the top view, the shutter release button is slightly visible from the front. This is the primary button used for taking photos, conveniently placed for easy access during operation.

12. **Self-Timer Indicator Light**
    - Near the lens, there is a small indicator light that signals when the self-timer function is in use. This is helpful for group shots or self-portraits, giving you visual feedback before the camera captures the image.

13. **Lens Hood Bayonet Mount**
    - Around the lens, the bayonet mount is used for attaching the included lens hood. This helps to block stray light from entering the lens, reducing lens flare and improving contrast, especially in bright outdoor shooting environments.

14. **Metal Body Design**
    - The camera features a high-quality metal construction that gives it a premium, durable feel. The sleek design combines modern technology with Leica's classic aesthetic, providing a professional look that stands out in the compact camera segment.

15. **Cooling Vents (Hidden)**
    - While not immediately visible, some cooling vents are subtly integrated into the camera's design. These help in dissipating heat generated during extended video

recording sessions or intensive shooting to keep the camera functioning optimally.

These features enhance the front view of the Leica D-Lux (Typ 109), combining both functional elements that support shooting performance and design choices that reflect Leica's high standards of craftsmanship and usability.

Rear View Layout

The **rear view layout** of the **Leica D-Lux (Typ 109)** is designed to provide easy access to key controls and features, ensuring smooth operation for both photographers and videographers. Here's a detailed breakdown of the key elements on the back of the camera:

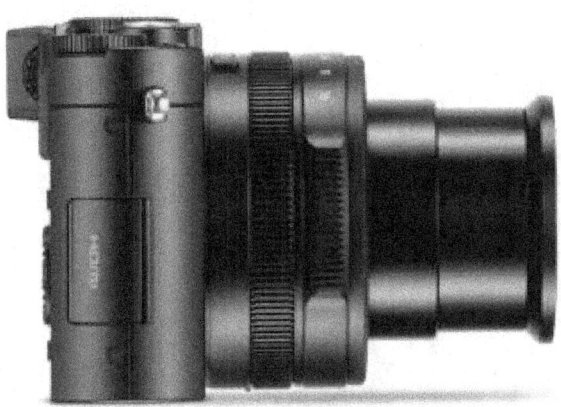

1. **High-Resolution Electronic Viewfinder (EVF)**

    o The EVF, located at the top centre, features a 2.76 million-dot resolution, providing a clear, sharp view for precise framing and focusing, even in bright outdoor conditions. It also includes an eye sensor that automatically switches between the EVF and the rear display when your eye is near.

2. **3.0-inch LCD Monitor**

    o Below the EVF, the 3.0-inch fixed LCD monitor offers a 921,000-dot resolution. It is bright and clear, making it ideal for live view shooting, navigating menus, and reviewing images and videos. The screen is not vari-angle but provides enough flexibility for most shooting conditions.

3. **Playback Button**

    o Positioned on the upper left corner of the LCD screen, this button allows you to enter playback mode to view your captured photos and videos. You can scroll through images, zoom in to check details, or delete files as needed.

4. **Menu/Set Button**
    - Located near the centre of the rear panel, this button opens the main menu where users can adjust various camera settings, from shooting modes to connectivity options. It also acts as a confirmation button when selecting options.

5. **Four-Way Control Pad (D-Pad)**
    - Surrounding the Menu/Set button, the D-pad is used for navigating the camera's menus and settings. Each directional button can be customized for quick access to commonly used functions like ISO, white balance, focus mode, and drive mode. The centre button serves as an additional "set" or "confirm" control.

6. **Fn Button (Function Button)**
    - Located next to the viewfinder, this customizable button can be assigned to various camera functions such as switching between RAW and JPEG image formats, controlling focus settings, or enabling Wi-Fi.

7. **Display (DISP) Button**
    - Below the D-pad, this button allows you to change the information displayed on the screen while shooting or during playback. You can toggle between different overlays, such as gridlines, histograms, and exposure details.

8. **Exposure Compensation Dial**
    - Positioned on the top right of the rear panel, this dial allows you to quickly adjust the exposure compensation (+/-) to brighten or darken your images without diving into the menu. It's a key feature for making quick exposure adjustments in varying lighting conditions.

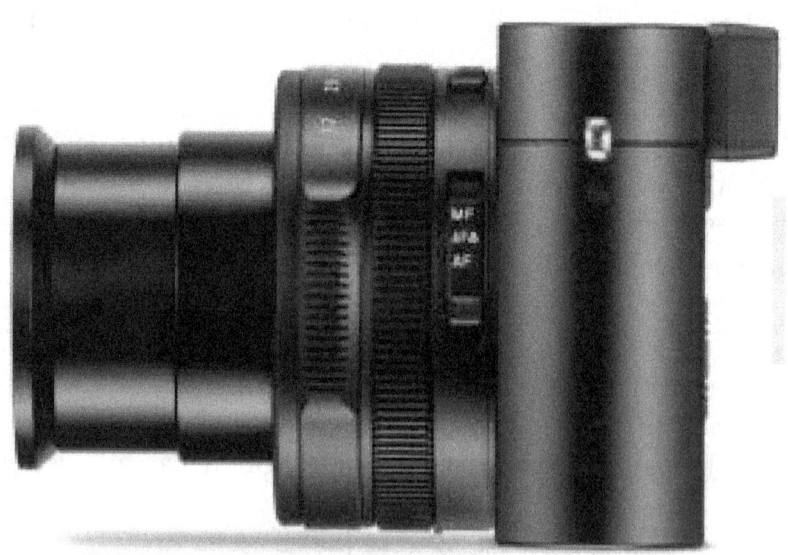

9. **AF/AE Lock Button**
    - Located just to the right of the viewfinder, this button locks focus and/or exposure when pressed, giving you more control over shooting in difficult lighting or focusing situations.

10. **Video Record Button**

- A dedicated button near the top right corner allows for instant video recording, making it easy to start and stop video capture without changing shooting modes.

11. **Zoom Lever (for Playback)**

- Surrounding the video record button, this lever is used for zooming in and out on photos during playback. It can also be used to switch between multi-image views or zoom into specific details within a single image.

12. **Q (Quick Menu) Button**

- Located to the right of the LCD, this button provides quick access to frequently used settings like ISO, white balance, drive mode, and focus mode. It's a customizable shortcut for fast adjustments while shooting.

13. **Diopter Adjustment Wheel**

- Found next to the EVF, this wheel allows you to adjust the viewfinder's focus according to your eyesight, ensuring a sharp and clear view while using the EVF.

14. **Wi-Fi Indicator**

- A small indicator light that confirms when Wi-Fi is enabled or when the camera is connecting to other devices wirelessly.

15. **Speaker Grill**

- Located near the bottom of the rear panel, this grill houses the built-in speaker for audio playback during video review or when navigating the menu system.

Additional Details:

- The rear panel of the Leica D-Lux (Typ 109) is compact, but intuitively designed to provide direct access to essential shooting and playback functions. The arrangement of buttons and dials ensures that users can make adjustments quickly, without removing their eye from the viewfinder or screen for too long.

This layout reflects Leica's focus on functionality and ease of use, giving photographers full control while shooting.

Top View Layout

The **top view layout** of the **Leica D-Lux (Typ 109)** is designed for intuitive operation, with easy access to key controls for both beginners and experienced photographers. Here's a breakdown of the top view features:

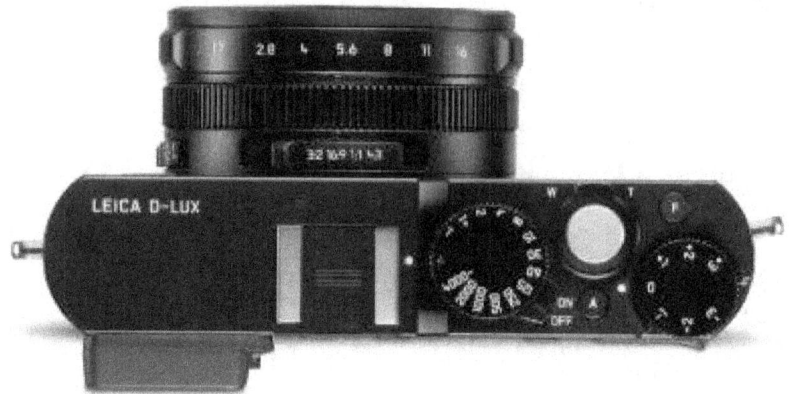

1. **Shutter Release Button**

    o Positioned at the front right, this button is the primary control for capturing images. It is slightly raised and responsive, allowing for a half-press to lock focus and exposure, and a full press to take the shot.

2. **Power Switch (On/Off)**

    o Surrounding the shutter release button, the power switch turns the camera on and off with a simple flick. Its proximity to the shutter button allows for quick startup and immediate readiness to shoot.

3. **Mode Dial**

    o Located near the right side, the mode dial allows you to switch between various shooting modes such as:

    - **P (Program Auto)**
    - **A (Aperture Priority)**
    - **S (Shutter Priority)**
    - **M (Manual)**
    - **SCN (Scene Mode)**
    - **C (Custom Mode)** The mode dial offers a tactile click when rotating, giving users direct access to different shooting styles without needing to navigate menus.

4. **Video Record Button**

    o Situated near the mode dial, this dedicated button allows users to start and stop video recording instantly, making it easier to switch from stills to video without changing settings.

5. **Hot Shoe Mount**
   - Positioned centrally at the top, this mount allows for the attachment of external accessories like flash units or external microphones. It is also covered by a protective hot shoe cover when not in use.

6. **Exposure Compensation Dial**
   - To the left of the hot shoe, this dial allows users to adjust exposure compensation between +3 and -3 stops. This is crucial for fine-tuning brightness in challenging lighting conditions, offering quick access to overexpose or underexpose images.

7. **Built-in Flash Pop-Up Switch**
   - Located just beside the hot shoe, this switch controls the built-in pop-up flash. When pressed, the flash pops up and is ready to use for low-light photography.

8. **Zoom Lever**
   - Surrounding the shutter release button, this lever is used for adjusting the zoom of the lens. Moving the lever left or right smoothly zooms in or out, controlling the focal length during shooting.

9. **Microphone Ports**
   - Located near the hot shoe, small microphone holes are integrated into the top of the camera for capturing audio during video recording. These built-in microphones provide stereo sound.

10. **Camera Strap Mounts**

- Two small metal loops are found at the far ends of the top view, allowing users to attach a camera strap for easy carrying. These mounts are sturdy, ensuring the camera is securely attached when using a neck or wrist strap.

The top view of the Leica D-Lux (Typ 109) is sleek and minimalistic, with all critical controls easily accessible for shooting on the go. The layout focuses on delivering a balance of manual control and automatic features, ensuring that photographers can quickly adjust settings while shooting.

Buttons and Controls

The **Leica D-Lux (Typ 109)** offers a well-organized array of buttons and controls designed to provide photographers with easy access to key functions while maintaining a compact form. Here's a detailed breakdown of the buttons and controls:

1. Shutter Release Button

- **Location:** Top right of the camera body
- **Function:** The primary button for capturing photos. Half-press to focus and full-press to take the shot. Surrounds the zoom lever for adjusting focal length.

2. Power Switch

- **Location:** Around the shutter release button
- **Function:** Controls the camera's power. Flick it on or off to power up or shut down the device. Positioned for quick operation.

3. Mode Dial

- **Location:** Top right, next to the shutter release button
- **Function:** Allows the user to select different shooting modes, such as:
    - **P (Program Mode)**
    - **A (Aperture Priority)**
    - **S (Shutter Priority)**
    - **M (Manual)**
    - **Scene Mode (SCN)**
    - **Custom Mode (C)**

4. Exposure Compensation Dial

- **Location:** Top left, near the hot shoe
- **Function:** Adjusts exposure compensation from +3 to -3 stops. This lets the user brighten or darken images without changing other exposure settings.

5. Video Record Button

- **Location:** Near the mode dial on the top right
- **Function:** A dedicated button for starting and stopping video recording, without having to switch from photo mode.

6. Flash Pop-Up Switch

- **Location:** Top near the hot shoe mount
- **Function:** Activates the built-in pop-up flash for low-light shooting situations.

7. Four-Way Control Pad (D-Pad)

- **Location:** Rear, surrounding the Menu/Set button
- **Function:** Used for navigating the camera's menu system and quickly accessing key functions:
    - **Up:** Quick access to ISO settings
    - **Down:** Direct access to drive modes (single, burst, timer)
    - **Left:** Focus settings (AF/MF toggle)
    - **Right:** White balance control

- ○ **Centre button (Set):** Confirms menu selections or setting changes.

8. Menu/Set Button

- **Location:** Centre of the D-pad on the rear of the camera
- **Function:** Accesses the main camera menu for adjusting settings, and also serves as the "enter" or confirmation button in menu navigation.

9. Q (Quick Menu) Button

- **Location:** To the right of the LCD screen on the rear panel
- **Function:** Opens a customizable quick menu where users can access commonly used settings such as ISO, white balance, and focus mode.

10. Playback Button

- **Location:** Rear, top left above the LCD screen
- **Function:** Enters playback mode to review captured images and videos.

11. Fn (Function) Button

- **Location:** Rear, next to the EVF
- **Function:** This is a customizable button that can be assigned to frequently used functions like Wi-Fi activation, RAW shooting toggle, or exposure lock.

12. AF/AE Lock Button

- **Location:** Rear, near the EVF
- **Function:** Locks focus (AF) and/or exposure (AE) when pressed, useful for recomposing shots after focusing.

13. Display (DISP) Button

- **Location:** Rear, below the D-pad
- **Function:** Toggles between different display options on the LCD screen, such as gridlines, histogram, and camera settings overlay.

14. Zoom Lever

- **Location:** Surrounding the shutter release button
- **Function:** Adjusts the zoom of the built-in lens. Moving the lever right zooms in, and left zooms out.

15. Electronic Viewfinder (EVF) Diopter Adjustment Wheel

- **Location:** Rear, next to the EVF
- **Function:** Adjusts the focus of the EVF to match the user's eyesight, ensuring a clear view for users with different vision.

16. Wi-Fi Button

- **Location:** Rear, near the top control buttons
- **Function:** Activates the built-in Wi-Fi for wireless sharing or remote control via a mobile device.

17. Lens Control Ring

- **Location:** Around the base of the lens
- **Function:** A customizable manual ring used to adjust focus, aperture, or zoom settings based on user preferences. Offers tactile control for precision adjustments.

Additional Controls:

- **Hot Shoe Mount:** Located at the top for attaching external accessories such as an external flash or microphone.
- **Lens Hood Attachment (Optional):** The front of the lens has a bayonet mount for attaching a lens hood to prevent flare.

These buttons and controls are designed for ease of access, allowing users to adjust settings quickly while shooting, providing both automatic and manual control over the camera's functions.

CHAPTER THREE
GETTING STARTED

Charging the Battery

Charging the battery of the **Leica D-Lux 8** is designed to be user-friendly, utilizing a USB-C connection for in-camera charging. Here are the key points regarding the battery charging process:

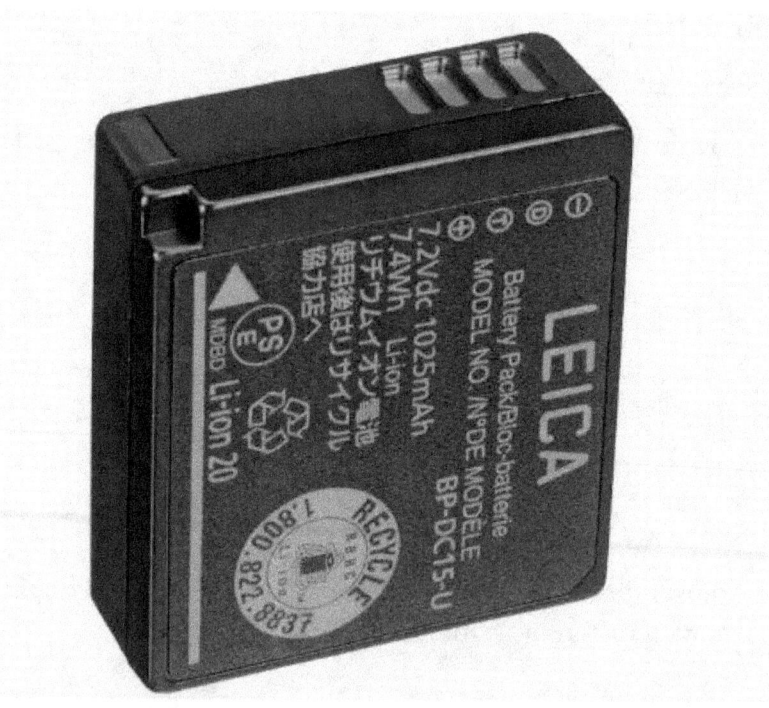

Battery Specifications
- **Battery Type**: The D-Lux 8 uses the **Leica BP-DC15**, a rechargeable lithium-ion battery.
- **Voltage and Capacity**: It operates at **7.2V** with a capacity of **1025mAh**. This battery is also compatible with the D-Lux 7 and Panasonic LX100 models.

Charging Process
- **In-Camera Charging**: The camera supports internal charging via the USB-C port. This allows users to charge the battery directly in the camera without needing a separate charger, which is convenient for travel.
- **Power Requirements**: When charging, the camera should be switched off. The USB-C port provides power input at **5V/1500mA** (2.5W or greater) for effective charging.
- **Data Transfer**: Initially, there were concerns that the USB-C connector was for power only, but it can also function for data transfer, allowing users to connect the camera to a computer for file transfer.

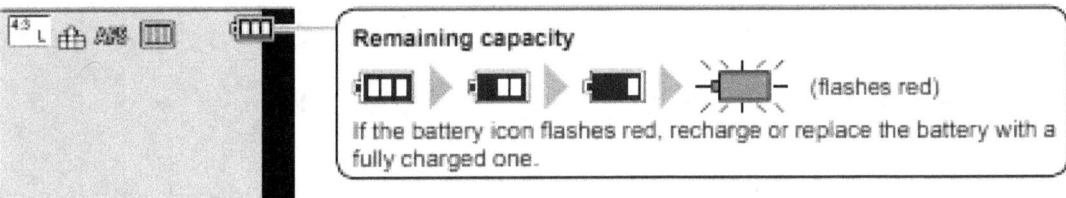

Battery Life
- The battery life is rated for approximately **240 shots** when using the electronic viewfinder (EVF) and **300 shots** with the LCD screen. However, real-world usage may yield fewer shots, and users are advised to carry extra batteries for extended shooting sessions.

In summary, the Leica D-Lux 8 offers a convenient USB-C charging option, making it easy to keep the battery charged while on the go, although users should be mindful of its average battery life.

Inserting the Battery and Memory Card
Inserting the Battery
1. Open the battery/memory card compartment door on the bottom of the camera.
2. Insert the Leica BP-DC15 lithium-ion battery, ensuring the contacts are facing the correct direction. The battery should slide in and lock into place.
3. Close the compartment door securely.

The BP-DC15 battery is rated at 7.2V DC and has a capacity of 1025mAh. It is identical to the battery used in the D-Lux 7 and Panasonic LX100 models, so third-party options are widely available.

Inserting the Memory Card
1. With the camera turned off, open the battery/memory card compartment door.

2. Insert a UHS-I or UHS-II SDHC/SDXC memory card into the single card slot, making sure the gold contacts are facing the correct direction. Push the card in until it clicks into place.

3. Close the compartment door.

The D-Lux 8 supports SD, SDHC and SDXC cards up to 2TB capacity. Leica recommends using a UHS-II card for optimal performance, especially when recording 4K video. A few important tips:

- **Never remove the memory card** while the camera is saving or accessing data, as this can corrupt the card and images.

- **Keep memory cards out of reach of children** to avoid swallowing hazards.

- **Avoid touching the card contacts** and keep them clean and dry.

- **Use a high-speed card rated for at least 90MB/s write speed** for 4K video recording without issues.

With the battery and card inserted, the D-Lux 8 is ready to power on and start capturing images and video. Just be sure to charge the battery fully before first use.

Powering On/Off
Powering on and off the **Leica D-Lux 8** involves a straightforward process that is designed to be intuitive for users. Here's a detailed guide on how to effectively manage the power functions of the camera:

Powering On
1. **Locate the Power Button**: The power button is situated to the right of the shutter release button on the top plate of the camera.

2. **Press the Power Button**: To turn on the camera, simply press the power button. A short press will activate the camera, and you will see the lens extend as the camera powers up.

3. **Wait for Initialization**: After pressing the power button, there may be a brief moment while the camera initializes. The display will light up, and the camera will be ready for use shortly thereafter.

4. **Using the Camera**: Once powered on, you can start taking photos or adjusting settings immediately. The camera will also automatically switch to the last used shooting mode.

Powering Off

1. **Press the Power Button Again**: To turn off the camera, press the power button once more. This action will retract the lens and power down the camera.

2. **Automatic Power Off Feature**: The D-Lux 8 has an automatic power-off feature that can be configured in the settings. By default, the camera will turn off after a period of inactivity (ranging from one to ten minutes). This feature is designed to conserve battery life.

3. **Disabling Auto Power Off**: If you prefer that the camera does not turn off automatically, you can disable this feature in the camera's menu settings. This setting allows the camera to remain powered on until you manually turn it off, similar to other Leica models.

Considerations

- **Soft Power Button**: Unlike previous models with a physical lever, the D-Lux 8 uses a soft power button. This design can lead to accidental power-offs if the button is inadvertently pressed while handling the camera.

- **Muscle Memory**: Users transitioning from other Leica models may need to adjust to the new button layout, as the power button's position can lead to confusion, especially when trying to take a shot quickly.

- **Startup Time**: The D-Lux 8 has a relatively quick startup time, but if the camera has powered off due to inactivity, it will require pressing the power button and waiting for the initialization process to complete before shooting.

In summary, powering on and off the Leica D-Lux 8 is a simple process, but users should be aware of the automatic power-off feature and the soft button design to avoid unintended shutdowns.

Setting Up Date and Time

To set up the date and time on the **Leica D-Lux 8**, follow these detailed steps:

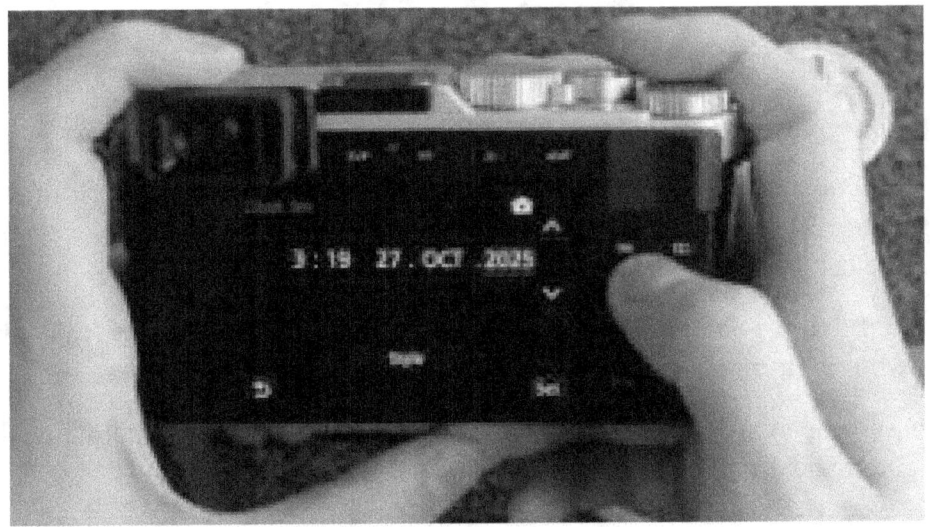

Setting Up Date and Time

1. **Power On the Camera**: Press the power button located on the top plate of the camera to turn it on.

2. **Access the Menu**: Press the **Menu** button to enter the main menu interface.

3. **Navigate to Camera Settings**: Use the directional pad or touchscreen to scroll through the menu options. Select **Camera Settings**.

4. **Select Date & Time**: Within the Camera Settings menu, find and select the **Date & Time** option.

5. **Adjust Date & Time Settings**:

   - **Select Date & Time Settings**: Choose this option to enter the date and time configuration screen.

   - **Set the Time Format**: You can choose between a 12-hour or 24-hour format. Select your preference.

   - **Set the Time**: Adjust the hour and minute. If you selected the 12-hour format, you will also need to select AM or PM.

   - **Set the Date**: Choose the desired date format (Day/Month/Year, Month/Day/Year, or Year/Month/Day) and enter the current date.

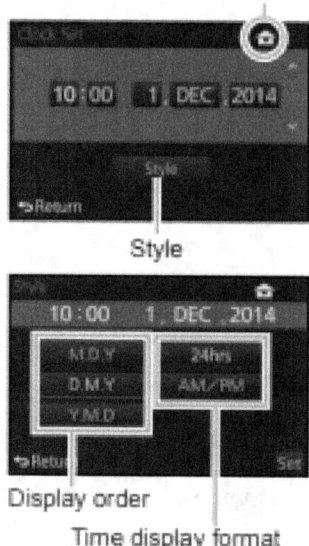

6. **Select Time Zone**: After setting the date and time, you can also set your time zone. This option is usually found in the same menu. Select your current location or time zone from the list provided.

7. **Enable Daylight Saving Time (if applicable)**: If your region observes daylight saving time, you can turn this feature on or off in the same settings menu.

8. **Save Settings**: Once you have made all your adjustments, exit the menu. The camera will automatically save your settings.

9. **Confirm Settings**: To ensure that the date and time are set correctly, you can take a test shot and check the EXIF data of the image, which will display the date and time the photo was taken.

Additional Notes

- **Battery Life**: Ensure that the battery is charged, as low battery levels may affect the camera's ability to save settings.
- **Resetting Date & Time**: If the camera is reset to factory settings or if the battery is removed for an extended period, you may need to repeat this process to set the date and time again.

By following these steps, you can easily configure the date and time settings on your Leica D-Lux 8, ensuring that your photos are accurately timestamped for future reference.

Setting the Language

Setting the language on the **Leica D-Lux 8** is a straightforward process. Here's a step-by-step guide to help you navigate through the settings and select your preferred language:

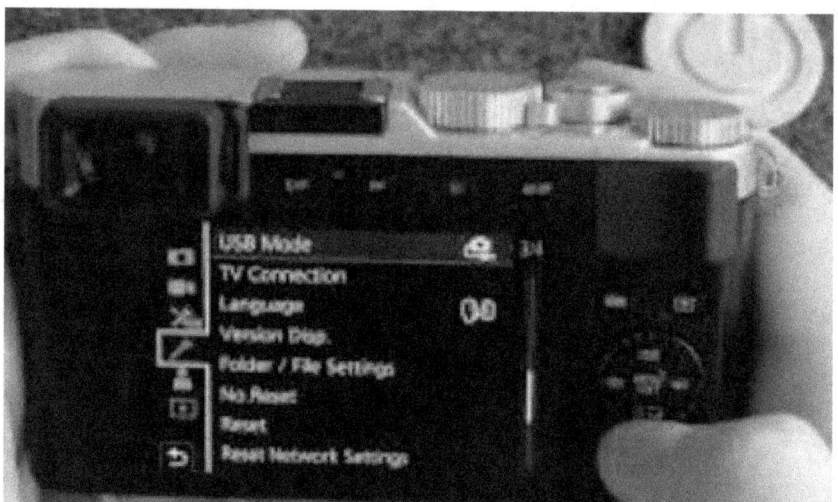

Setting the Language

1. **Power On the Camera**: Press the power button located on the top plate of the camera to turn it on.

2. **Access the Menu**: Press the **Menu** button to enter the main menu interface.

3. **Navigate to Settings**: Use the directional pad or touchscreen to scroll through the menu options. Look for the **Setup** or **Settings** icon, which typically resembles a wrench or gear.

4. **Select Language**: Within the Setup or Settings menu, find and select the **Language** option. This may be represented by a globe icon or simply labeled as "Language."

5. **Choose Your Preferred Language**: A list of available languages will be displayed. Use the directional pad or touchscreen to scroll through the options. Highlight your desired language and press the **OK** or **Select** button to confirm your choice.

6. **Exit the Menu**: After selecting the language, you can exit the menu by pressing the **Menu** button again or by pressing the **OK** button to return to the main shooting interface.

7. **Confirm Language Change**: The camera interface will now display all menus and settings in the selected language. You can take a moment to familiarize yourself with the new language settings.

Additional Notes

- **Default Language**: The camera is typically set to a default language (usually English) upon first use. If you purchase a model in a different region, the default language may vary.

- **Changing Language Again**: If you ever need to change the language again, simply follow the same steps outlined above.

- **User Manual**: If you are unsure about any of the options or need further assistance, refer to the user manual provided with your camera, which will detail the language settings and other features.

By following these steps, you can easily set the language on your Leica D-Lux 8, ensuring that you can navigate the camera's menus and settings comfortably in your preferred language.

CHAPTER FOUR
BASIC OPERATION

Auto Mode Overview

The Auto Mode on the Leica D-Lux (Typ 109) is designed to simplify photography for users who want to capture high-quality images without manually adjusting the camera settings. In this mode, the camera automatically selects the optimal settings based on the scene it detects, allowing photographers to focus entirely on composition and timing. Here's an overview of how Auto Mode works:

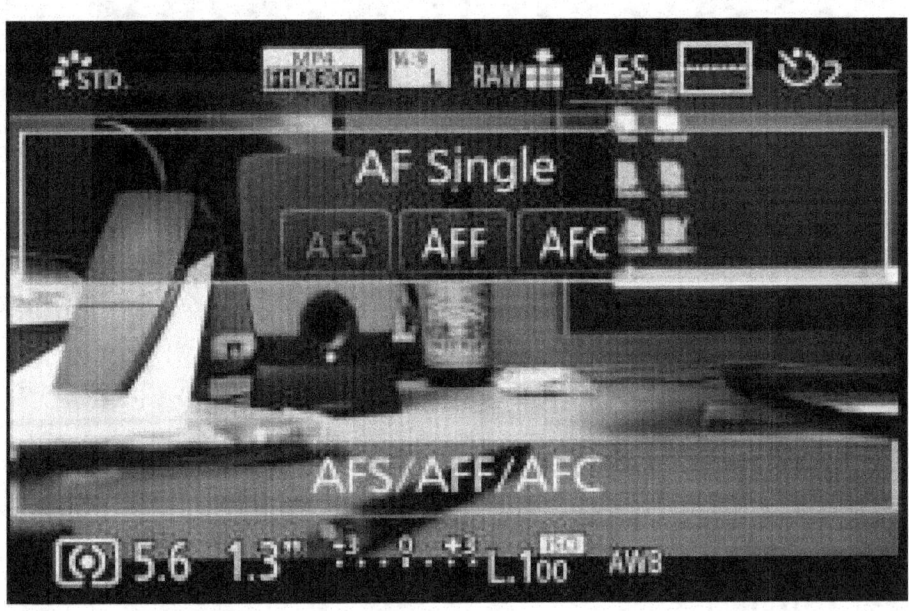

1. Automatic Scene Detection

- In Auto Mode, the camera uses advanced algorithms to detect the type of scene being photographed (e.g., portrait, landscape, macro, night, etc.). Based on this detection, it adjusts parameters such as:
    - **Exposure (Shutter Speed, Aperture, ISO)**
    - **White Balance**
    - **Focus Mode**
    - **Metering Mode**
- This ensures that the camera captures well-exposed and properly focused images without user intervention.

2. Autofocus

- The Leica D-Lux (Typ 109) automatically selects the appropriate autofocus (AF) mode in Auto Mode, choosing between **single AF**, **continuous AF**, or **face detection** depending on the scene. This helps to ensure that subjects are always in focus, especially in dynamic environments or for moving subjects.

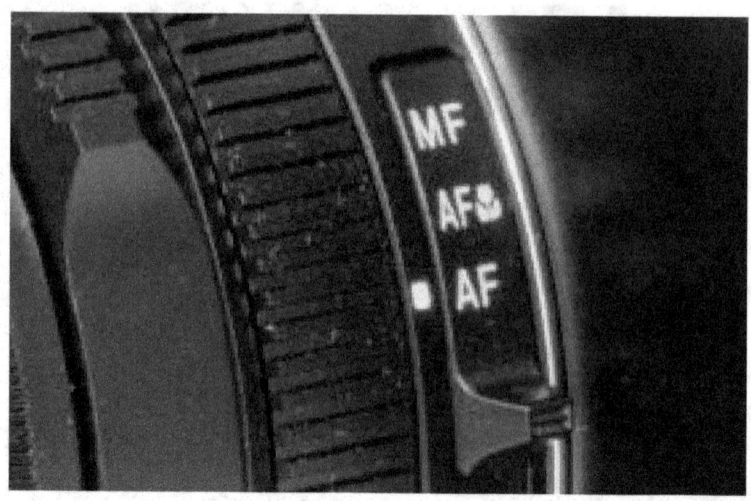

3. Intelligent ISO Setting

- Auto Mode automatically adjusts the ISO sensitivity based on the available light. In low-light conditions, the camera increases the ISO to maintain an appropriate shutter speed and avoid motion blur. In brighter scenes, the ISO is reduced to ensure the best image quality with minimal noise.

4. Automatic White Balance

- The camera determines the best white balance setting depending on the lighting conditions, ensuring that colours are accurate and natural regardless of the light source (e.g., sunlight, fluorescent, incandescent).

5. Built-in Flash Activation

- If the camera detects low-light conditions, it will automatically activate the built-in pop-up flash. The camera decides whether flash is necessary and adjusts the flash output accordingly to avoid overexposure.

6. Exposure Compensation Adjustment

- While Auto Mode generally takes full control of exposure settings, users can still apply **exposure compensation** using the dedicated dial on the top of the camera. This allows minor adjustments to make the image brighter or darker depending on user preference.

7. Face and Eye Detection

- Auto Mode uses **face and eye detection** technology to automatically focus on faces in the frame. This ensures that portraits and group shots are always sharp, with a special emphasis on the eyes.

8. Image Stabilization

- The Leica D-Lux (Typ 109) features built-in optical image stabilization (OIS), which is especially useful in Auto Mode. The camera automatically engages stabilization when it detects slower shutter speeds or camera movement, helping to minimize blur caused by shaky hands.

9. JPEG Output

- In Auto Mode, images are generally saved in **JPEG format**, with the camera applying optimal image processing to enhance colour, contrast, and sharpness. The user can still access RAW capture, but Auto Mode prioritizes JPEG for quick and easy results.

10. Auto ISO and Shutter Speed Limits

- The camera sets the minimum shutter speed and adjusts the ISO accordingly to avoid motion blur in situations where the user or the subject is in motion. This allows for sharper images even without manual adjustments.

11. Auto Focus Mode Switching

- Depending on the subject, the camera can switch between **single-point AF** (for still subjects), **tracking AF** (for moving subjects), or **multi-area AF** (for general scenes), ensuring that the subject is always in focus.

12. Macro Mode Activation

- When the camera detects that the subject is close to the lens, it automatically switches to **macro mode**, allowing for detailed close-up shots without requiring manual input from the user.

13. Silent Shooting

- In some situations, Auto Mode may activate **silent shooting** (disabling shutter noise) to allow for discreet photography, such as in quiet environments or when shooting candid moments.

Benefits of Auto Mode:

- **Ease of Use:** Auto Mode is perfect for beginners or casual photographers who want to focus on the moment rather than on technical settings.
- **Fast Response:** The camera quickly adapts to changing lighting and shooting conditions, ensuring you don't miss a shot due to manual adjustment delays.
- **Reliability:** Leica's intelligent scene detection ensures that most settings are optimal, producing consistently high-quality results across various scenarios.
- **Convenience:** Auto Mode is ideal for situations where you need to shoot quickly, like street photography, travel, or spontaneous events.

When to Use Auto Mode:

- **Travel Photography:** When you need to capture spontaneous moments without worrying about adjusting camera settings.
- **Family or Group Photos:** Auto Mode ensures faces are in focus and well-exposed.
- **Low-Light Situations:** The camera automatically manages ISO and flash to optimize exposure in dim conditions.
- **General Photography:** Perfect for users who want to point and shoot with minimal setup while still achieving Leica-quality images.

In summary, Auto Mode on the Leica D-Lux (Typ 109) simplifies the shooting process, providing intelligent settings that adapt to the scene while still delivering the high-quality images expected from a Leica camera.

Shutter Release Button

The Shutter Release Button on the Leica D-Lux (Typ 109) is a central control that plays a crucial role in capturing images. Its design and functionality ensure that both focusing and shooting are intuitive, providing a seamless experience for photographers.

Here's a detailed overview of its key functions:

1. Two-Step Mechanism

- The shutter release button has a **two-step function**:
    - **Half-Press:** When the button is pressed halfway, the camera locks focus and exposure. This allows you to compose your shot while ensuring that the subject is in focus and the exposure is correct.
    - **Full-Press:** Pressing the button fully captures the image. The transition from half-press to full-press is smooth, reducing the chance of camera shake and resulting in sharper images.

2. Autofocus Activation

- **Half-pressing** the shutter button also activates the autofocus (AF) system. Depending on the selected autofocus mode, the camera either locks focus on a single point (Single AF) or continuously tracks a moving subject (Continuous AF). This makes it easy to maintain focus on your subject before taking the shot.

3. Metering and Exposure Lock

- When the shutter release button is pressed halfway, the camera evaluates the scene and locks the exposure based on the selected **metering mode**. This is particularly useful when shooting in challenging lighting conditions, ensuring the correct exposure is maintained.

4. Burst Mode

- In burst mode, holding down the shutter release button allows the camera to capture a series of shots in quick succession. This is ideal for action photography or any situation where you want to capture multiple frames to choose from.

5. Silent Shooting

- The camera features a **silent shooting mode**, where the shutter sound is minimized, allowing for more discreet photography. This can be activated in settings and allows for silent operation, especially useful for shooting in quiet environments or capturing candid moments.

6. Responsiveness
- The shutter release button on the Leica D-Lux (Typ 109) is highly responsive, allowing for quick captures with minimal lag. This is critical for action shots or fast-paced environments where timing is everything.

7. Zoom Control Integration
- Surrounding the shutter release button is the **zoom lever**, which allows users to control the zoom range of the camera. This placement makes it easy to adjust zoom levels without moving your hand from the shutter button, enhancing shooting fluidity.

Key Features:
- **Ergonomic Placement:** The shutter release button is conveniently located on the top of the camera for easy access, ensuring comfortable use during long shoots.
- **Smooth Operation:** The tactile feel and smooth two-step action reduce the risk of camera shake, allowing for sharper images, especially in low-light conditions.
- **Quick Response:** Fast shutter response time ensures that you capture the shot exactly when you want, minimizing shutter lag.

Use Cases:
- **Portraits:** Half-press to lock focus on a subject's face and fully press to take the shot once composed.
- **Action Photography:** Use burst mode and hold down the button to capture multiple frames of fast-moving subjects.
- **Street Photography:** Silent shooting mode with the shutter release button allows for discreet captures in quiet or intimate environments.

The **shutter release button** is a fundamental part of the Leica D-Lux (Typ 109)'s user interface, providing intuitive and responsive control for capturing high-quality images.

Zooming

The Leica D-Lux (Typ 109) features a versatile zoom system that allows users to adjust the focal length of the lens to suit various shooting scenarios. The zooming capability is controlled primarily through the zoom lever located around the shutter release button.

1. Zoom Range
- The Leica D-Lux (Typ 109) is equipped with a **Leica DC Vario-Summilux 10.9–34 mm f/1.7–2.8 ASPH. lens**, which provides a **3.1x optical zoom**. In 35mm equivalent terms, this translates to a **24-75mm zoom range**.
    - **Wide Angle (24mm):** Ideal for landscapes, architecture, and wide group shots, allowing you to capture more of the scene.
    - **Telephoto (75mm):** Useful for portraits, close-ups, and bringing distant subjects closer without physically moving closer.

2. Zoom Lever Control

- The **zoom lever** is conveniently positioned around the shutter release button, allowing easy zooming while composing a shot.
    - **Push to the right** to zoom in (telephoto) and bring the subject closer.
    - **Push to the left** to zoom out (wide-angle) and capture more of the scene.
- This lever offers smooth control, allowing users to adjust zoom levels gradually or quickly, depending on the situation.

3. Optical Zoom vs. Digital Zoom

- **Optical Zoom:** The camera utilizes the full capacity of its lens to zoom without compromising image quality. With a 3.1x optical zoom, you get sharp and detailed images across the entire zoom range.
- **Digital Zoom:** Beyond the optical zoom range, the camera can engage digital zoom to further magnify the subject, but this may result in a loss of image quality. The camera offers up to **4x digital zoom**, extending the focal length significantly, but digital zoom is best used when necessary, as it crops and interpolates pixels.

4. Zoom in Video Mode

- When shooting video, the **zoom function** is fully operational. The camera provides **smooth zooming** without jerks, ensuring professional-quality video recording. Users can zoom in and out while recording, making it possible to adjust framing dynamically during the shot.

5. Macro Mode Zoom

- In **macro mode**, the camera allows you to zoom in close to subjects at very short distances (up to 3cm). This mode is ideal for detailed close-up shots, such as flowers, insects, or small objects. The zoom lever still functions in this mode but is designed for fine-tuned control.

6. Zoom Display on Screen

- As you zoom, the focal length is displayed on the LCD or electronic viewfinder (EVF), allowing you to see exactly what zoom level you are using. This is particularly helpful for ensuring precise composition and framing.

7. Step Zoom and Zoom Resume

- **Step Zoom:** This feature allows you to zoom in predefined steps (24mm, 35mm, 50mm, etc.), simulating the experience of using prime lenses. It provides more control for users who prefer specific focal lengths.
- **Zoom Resume:** After turning off the camera, it can remember the last zoom position and return to it when powered on again, ensuring continuity during a shooting session.

Use Cases for Zooming:

- **Portraits:** Use the telephoto end (around 75mm) for flattering close-ups with a natural perspective and background separation.

- **Landscape Photography:** Zoom out to wide-angle (24mm) for expansive scenes with more depth and detail.

- **Street Photography:** The mid-range (35mm to 50mm) is ideal for capturing street scenes and candid moments with a natural field of view.

- **Close-ups and Macro:** In macro mode, zoom in to capture intricate details at close range.

Key Features of Zooming:

- **Smooth Zoom Lever Operation:** Ergonomically placed for ease of use while shooting.

- **24-75mm Versatility:** Covers a wide range of focal lengths, making the camera highly adaptable to different subjects and shooting styles.

- **Macro Zooming:** Allows for close-up shots with detailed focus.

- **Digital Zoom:** Extends beyond optical zoom but is best used sparingly to maintain image quality.

The zooming feature on the Leica D-Lux (Typ 109) is both flexible and intuitive, offering precision control for various types of photography, from wide-angle landscapes to telephoto portraits and close-up details.

Capturing Images

The Leica D-Lux (Typ 109) is designed to provide a seamless image-capturing experience, combining intuitive controls with high-quality optics and advanced features. Here's a detailed guide on how the camera captures images and the key features involved:

1. Basic Capture Process

- **Step 1:** Compose the shot using either the **electronic viewfinder (EVF)** or the **LCD display**.

- **Step 2:** Use the **zoom lever** to adjust focal length as needed.

- **Step 3: Half-press** the **shutter release button** to activate autofocus (AF) and lock exposure. The camera automatically selects focus points and adjusts settings for optimal exposure.

- **Step 4: Fully press** the shutter release button to take the picture.

2. Autofocus System

- The camera uses a **contrast-detection AF system** to ensure fast and accurate focus. There are various focus modes available, such as:

- **Single AF (AFS):** Focuses on a single point and locks focus when the shutter button is half-pressed.
- **Continuous AF (AFC):** Continuously adjusts focus while tracking a moving subject.
- **Face/Eye Detection:** The camera detects and focuses on faces and eyes, ideal for portraits.
- **Macro Mode:** For close-up shots, the camera switches to macro mode when it detects that the subject is very close to the lens.

3. Image Formats

- The camera supports both **JPEG** and **RAW** image formats:
    - **JPEG:** The camera processes and compresses the image, making it ready for immediate sharing and viewing.
    - **RAW:** Provides unprocessed image data, offering more flexibility for post-processing with advanced photo-editing software.
- You can choose to shoot in JPEG, RAW, or both simultaneously.

4. Exposure Settings

- In **Auto Mode**, the camera automatically sets the optimal exposure by adjusting shutter speed, aperture, and ISO sensitivity based on the scene.
- In **Manual Mode** and other semi-automatic modes (P, A, S), you have full control over the exposure settings:
    - **Aperture:** Controls the depth of field and is manually adjustable via the lens ring.
    - **Shutter Speed:** Adjusts how long the sensor is exposed to light, affecting motion blur.
    - **ISO:** Controls the sensor's sensitivity to light, with higher values used for low-light environments.

5. Shooting Modes

- The Leica D-Lux (Typ 109) offers various shooting modes to suit different scenarios:
    - **Auto Mode:** Fully automatic, where the camera determines the optimal settings.
    - **P (Program Mode):** The camera selects shutter speed and aperture while allowing you to control other settings like ISO and white balance.
    - **A (Aperture Priority):** You select the aperture, and the camera adjusts the shutter speed.
    - **S (Shutter Priority):** You control the shutter speed, and the camera selects the aperture.

- o **M (Manual Mode):** Full manual control over both aperture and shutter speed.
- o **Scene Modes:** Predefined settings for specific scenes like portraits, landscapes, and night photography.

6. Burst Mode (Continuous Shooting)

- In **burst mode**, the camera captures multiple images in quick succession by holding down the shutter release button. This is useful for action photography, where you want to capture a sequence of shots.
- The Leica D-Lux (Typ 109) can shoot at up to **11 frames per second (fps)** in burst mode.

7. Image Stabilization

- The camera is equipped with **optical image stabilization (OIS)**, which compensates for camera shake, especially when shooting at slower shutter speeds or with a longer focal length. This helps produce sharper images, particularly in low-light situations or when hand-holding the camera.

8. Silent Mode

- The camera offers a **silent shooting mode**, where the electronic shutter is used instead of the mechanical one. This makes the camera completely silent during operation, ideal for discreet photography in quiet environments or events.

9. Manual Focus

- For greater control, you can switch to **manual focus** using the focus ring on the lens. The camera provides **focus peaking**, which highlights the in-focus areas of the image, making it easier to achieve precise focus.

10. Custom Settings

- The camera allows you to save your preferred settings as **custom modes (C1, C2)**, so you can quickly switch to your favourite shooting configurations.

11. Self-Timer and Remote Capture

- The camera has a **self-timer** function (2s or 10s), useful for group shots or self-portraits.
- You can also use the Leica D-Lux (Typ 109)'s **Wi-Fi capabilities** to remotely capture images using a smartphone or tablet, giving you more flexibility when composing shots from a distance.

Use Cases for Capturing Images:

- **Portrait Photography:** Use face and eye detection for sharp, well-exposed portraits. The wide aperture (f/1.7-2.8) allows for beautiful background blur (bokeh).
- **Street and Travel Photography:** The compact size and fast autofocus make it ideal for capturing spontaneous moments. Use burst mode to capture fast-paced scenes.

- **Landscape Photography:** Use aperture priority or manual mode to control depth of field and ensure sharpness across the frame. The wide-angle lens (24mm) is great for expansive views.

- **Low-Light Photography:** The fast aperture and image stabilization help in dimly lit environments without needing a tripod or external flash.

Key Features of Capturing Images:

- **High-Speed Performance:** Up to 11 fps burst shooting for action and sports photography.

- **Fast Autofocus:** Accurate and quick focusing, even in challenging lighting conditions.

- **RAW and JPEG Support:** Offers flexibility in post-processing with RAW and instant sharing with JPEG.

- **Versatile Shooting Modes:** A range of automatic and manual modes cater to all levels of photographers.

The **Leica D-Lux (Typ 109)** is a versatile camera that combines ease of use with powerful features, making it an excellent choice for photographers who want high-quality images in various shooting conditions.

Playback Mode

The **Playback Mode** on the **Leica D-Lux (Typ 109)** allows you to view and manage the photos and videos you have captured. It offers a variety of features for reviewing, zooming in on details, deleting, and organizing images, ensuring that you can easily assess and manage your work.

1. Accessing Playback Mode

- To enter **Playback Mode**, press the **Playback button** (marked with a play icon) located on the rear of the camera.

- This allows you to review the most recent photo or video captured, and you can navigate through the rest of the media using the **directional pad** or **control dial**.

2. Image Review Options

- You can scroll through your images and videos by:
  - Using the **left and right buttons** on the directional pad to move between individual images.
  - Rotating the **control dial** to quickly move through a larger number of images.

- Images can be displayed one at a time or in a **thumbnail view** (accessible via the zoom out control), which shows a grid of images for faster navigation through your photo library.

3. Zooming in on Images

- To inspect details, you can zoom in on a photo during playback:
    - **Rotate the zoom lever** to zoom in (up to 16x magnification).
    - Once zoomed in, use the **directional buttons** to move around the image and inspect different areas.
- This is particularly useful for checking sharpness, focus, or fine details in critical parts of the image.

4. Deleting Images

- Images or videos can be deleted directly in Playback Mode:
    - Press the **Delete button** (marked with a trash can icon) to remove the selected photo or video.
    - The camera will prompt you to confirm the deletion, offering options like:
        - **Delete Single**: Removes only the currently selected image or video.
        - **Delete All**: Deletes all images on the memory card (use with caution).
- This helps free up storage space while reviewing shots in the field.

5. Playback for Videos

- When a video is selected in Playback Mode, press the **Set/OK button** to start playback.
- Use the **directional pad** to pause, resume, or skip forward/backward within the video.
- Audio from the video will be played through the camera's built-in speaker. You can adjust the volume using the directional buttons or control dial.

6. Slideshow Mode

- The camera offers a **slideshow feature**, allowing you to automatically display all photos and videos in sequence. You can set the interval time for how long each image is displayed.
- This is ideal for reviewing your captures without manually scrolling or for displaying images on a larger screen when connected via HDMI.

7. Rating and Protecting Images

- In Playback Mode, you can **rate** images (using a star system) for easier sorting and organizing later when transferring to a computer or editing software.
- You can also **protect images** from accidental deletion by selecting the protect option in the menu. Protected images will remain on the memory card until you manually remove the protection.

8. Playback Menu Options

- In Playback Mode, press the **Menu button** to access more detailed settings, such as:

- o **Slide Show Settings:** Customize the playback speed and order for slideshows.
- o **Copy to Card:** Copy images from one memory card to another (if using dual slots).
- o **Rotate Image:** Manually rotate an image if it was captured at an unusual angle.
- o **Create a Video from Photos:** Some advanced cameras allow for a short video montage using selected photos.

9. Image Information Display

- You can toggle the **information display** on and off by pressing the **Info button**. This can show a range of details about each image, such as:
    - o **File name**
    - o **Shooting date and time**
    - o **Aperture, shutter speed, ISO settings**
    - o **Histogram** (to check exposure distribution)
    - o **Focus point** used during capture

10. Playback on External Devices

- The Leica D-Lux (Typ 109) can be connected to a TV or external monitor using the **HDMI output**. This allows you to view your images and videos on a larger screen.
- You can also transfer images to a smartphone or tablet using the **Wi-Fi connection**, enabling remote playback or sharing to social media directly from your mobile device.

Key Features of Playback Mode:

- **Zoom In/Out:** Magnify images up to 16x to check details or zoom out for a thumbnail view.
- **Slideshow:** Display all images in a sequence, perfect for presentations or reviewing multiple shots.
- **Delete Options:** Easily remove unwanted images or videos to free up space.
- **Rating & Protection:** Organize your images with ratings or protect them from accidental deletion.
- **Image Information:** View detailed metadata and exposure settings to evaluate your shot.

Use Cases for Playback Mode:

- **Checking Focus and Exposure:** Use zoom to inspect fine details and ensure your image is sharp and correctly exposed.
- **On-the-Go Culling:** Quickly delete unwanted shots while still in the field, keeping your memory card organized.

- **Creating a Visual Story:** Use the slideshow feature to showcase your photos in sequence, ideal for sharing with friends or family.
- **Post-Shooting Review:** Analyze your images by viewing the histogram and metadata to improve future shots.

The **Playback Mode** on the Leica D-Lux (Typ 109) is intuitive and offers a wide range of options for reviewing and managing images and videos, ensuring you have full control over your captured content.

CHAPTER FIVE
ADVANCED SHOOTING MODES

Aperture Priority Mode (A)

Aperture Priority Mode (A) on the Leica D-Lux (Typ 109) allows you to manually control the aperture (f-stop), while the camera automatically adjusts the shutter speed to maintain proper exposure. This mode is particularly useful for controlling **depth of field**, making it ideal for portraits, landscapes, and creative photography.

1. What is Aperture?

- The **aperture** refers to the opening in the lens through which light enters the camera. It is measured in **f-stops** (e.g., f/1.7, f/2.8, f/11), with smaller numbers representing a larger aperture (wider opening) and larger numbers representing a smaller aperture (narrower opening).

    - **Larger Aperture (e.g., f/1.7):** More light enters the camera, resulting in a **shallow depth of field**, where only the subject is in focus and the background is blurred (bokeh effect).

    - **Smaller Aperture (e.g., f/11):** Less light enters, creating a **deep depth of field**, where both the subject and background are in focus, ideal for landscape shots.

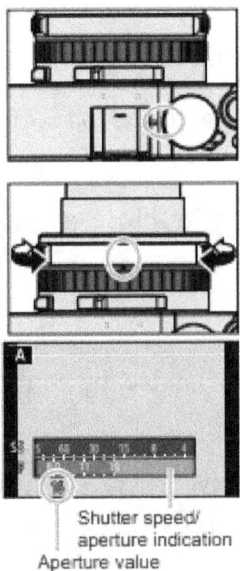

Shutter speed/
aperture indication
Aperture value

2. How to Use Aperture Priority Mode

- **Step 1:** Turn the **mode dial** to the **A (Aperture Priority)** setting.

- **Step 2:** Adjust the **aperture** by rotating the **aperture ring** on the lens. You'll see the f-stop value change on the screen or in the electronic viewfinder (EVF).

- **Step 3:** Compose your shot and half-press the **shutter release button** to focus and check exposure. The camera automatically selects the appropriate shutter speed based on the aperture you've chosen.

- **Step 4:** Fully press the shutter release to capture the image.

3. Advantages of Using Aperture Priority Mode

- **Control Over Depth of Field:**
    - A **wide aperture (f/1.7–2.8)** creates a shallow depth of field, isolating your subject from the background, which is perfect for portrait photography.
    - A **narrow aperture (f/8–f/11)** ensures that more of the scene is in focus, making it ideal for landscapes and architectural photography.
- **Faster Adjustments:** In **Aperture Priority Mode**, the camera handles the shutter speed, allowing you to focus on creative aspects like depth of field without worrying about exposure settings.

4. Aperture Control on Leica D-Lux (Typ 109)

- The Leica D-Lux (Typ 109) has a **Leica DC Vario-Summilux 10.9–34mm f/1.7–2.8 ASPH. lens**, which offers:
    - **Wide Aperture Range:** From f/1.7 (wide-angle) to f/2.8 (telephoto).
- This wide aperture range is ideal for low-light photography as it lets in more light, allowing for faster shutter speeds and minimizing the need for high ISO.

5. Depth of Field Control

- **Shallow Depth of Field (f/1.7–f/2.8):**
    - Use a wide aperture to blur the background, making the subject stand out sharply.
    - Perfect for portrait, macro, or close-up photography, where you want to isolate the subject.
- **Deep Depth of Field (f/8–f/11):**
    - Use a smaller aperture for landscape shots where you want both the foreground and background in focus.
    - This is useful in situations where capturing detail across the entire scene is important, such as nature photography.

6. Exposure Control

- Although the camera controls the **shutter speed**, you still have some control over exposure by adjusting the **exposure compensation**. This allows you to make the image brighter or darker without changing the aperture. Exposure compensation can be adjusted using the **control dial** or **dedicated exposure compensation button**.

7. Shutter Speed Considerations

- In low-light conditions, using a narrow aperture may result in slower shutter speeds, which could cause motion blur. You can:

- o **Increase ISO:** This makes the sensor more sensitive to light, allowing faster shutter speeds, but may introduce some noise.
- o **Use a Tripod:** A tripod stabilizes the camera and allows for long exposures without camera shake.
- Conversely, if shooting with a wide aperture (e.g., f/1.7) in bright conditions, the camera will automatically select faster shutter speeds to prevent overexposure.

8. Creative Applications

- **Portraits:** Select a wide aperture (e.g., f/1.7) to create a beautiful background blur (bokeh), making your subject pop against a soft, defocused background.
- **Landscapes:** Use a narrow aperture (e.g., f/8 or f/11) to ensure sharpness from the foreground to the background.
- **Macro Photography:** A wide aperture allows you to focus on tiny details while blurring out distracting backgrounds.
- **Low-Light Photography:** A wide aperture can help in low-light situations by allowing more light to hit the sensor, reducing the need for artificial lighting or flash.

9. Aperture and Lens Performance

- The Leica DC Vario-Summilux lens is known for its exceptional sharpness even at wide apertures, ensuring that your images remain crisp and vibrant throughout the aperture range.
- **Edge-to-edge sharpness** is maintained even at wider apertures, meaning that whether you shoot at f/1.7 or f/8, you'll still achieve high-quality results.

Use Cases for Aperture Priority Mode:

- **Portraits:** Use f/1.7–f/2.8 for beautiful bokeh, isolating your subject from the background.
- **Landscapes:** Use f/8–f/11 for maximum depth of field, ensuring sharpness across the entire frame.
- **Street Photography:** Aperture priority allows for quick adjustments to focus on capturing candid moments with the desired depth of field.

Key Features of Aperture Priority Mode (A):

- **Manual Control of Aperture:** Direct control over the f-stop setting for creative depth of field effects.
- **Automatic Shutter Speed:** The camera automatically selects the ideal shutter speed for correct exposure.
- **Exposure Compensation:** Adjust brightness and darkness without altering the aperture setting.
- **Fast and Easy Adjustments:** Ideal for quickly changing depth of field while letting the camera manage exposure.

In **Aperture Priority Mode**, the Leica D-Lux (Typ 109) gives photographers creative control over depth of field, allowing for striking portraits with soft backgrounds or detailed landscapes with sharp focus throughout the scene. The mode is perfect for those who want flexibility and creative control without worrying about the technicalities of shutter speed adjustments.

Shutter Priority Mode (S)

Shutter Priority Mode (S) on the Leica D-Lux (Typ 109) allows you to manually control the shutter speed, while the camera automatically adjusts the aperture to maintain proper exposure. This mode is particularly useful for capturing fast-moving subjects or controlling motion blur.

1. What is Shutter Speed?

- **Shutter speed** refers to the length of time the camera's shutter remains open to expose light onto the sensor. It is measured in seconds or fractions of a second (e.g., 1/500s, 1/60s, 2s).
    - **Fast Shutter Speed (e.g., 1/1000s):** Captures fast-moving subjects with minimal motion blur, ideal for action shots and sports photography.
    - **Slow Shutter Speed (e.g., 1/30s):** Allows more light to hit the sensor, which can create motion blur for moving subjects, or capture images in low-light conditions. This can also be used creatively to show motion or light trails.

2. How to Use Shutter Priority Mode

- **Step 1:** Turn the **mode dial** to **S (Shutter Priority)**.
- **Step 2:** Adjust the **shutter speed** using the **control dial** or **shutter speed dial** (if available).
- **Step 3:** Compose your shot and half-press the **shutter release button** to let the camera calculate the appropriate aperture for exposure.
- **Step 4:** Fully press the shutter release button to capture the image.

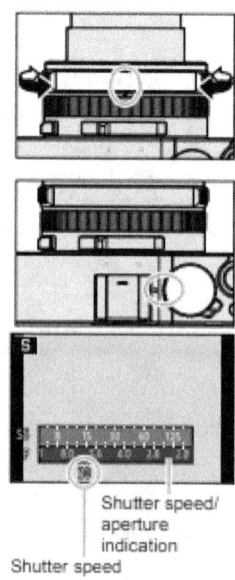

Shutter speed/aperture indication

Shutter speed

3. Advantages of Using Shutter Priority Mode

- **Control Over Motion Blur:**
    - Use a fast shutter speed to freeze motion and capture sharp, clear images of moving subjects.
    - Use a slow shutter speed to introduce intentional motion blur, such as creating a sense of movement or capturing light trails.
- **Dynamic Shots:** Ideal for action photography, sports, and creative long-exposure shots.

4. Shutter Speed Control on Leica D-Lux (Typ 109)

- The Leica D-Lux (Typ 109) offers a range of shutter speeds, from very fast (1/16000s) to slower speeds (up to 60s). This range allows you to capture both high-speed action and long-exposure effects.

5. Motion Blur and Freeze Motion

- **Freezing Motion:**
    - Use faster shutter speeds (e.g., 1/1000s or faster) to capture fast-moving subjects, such as athletes or wildlife, with minimal blur.
- **Creating Motion Blur:**
    - Use slower shutter speeds (e.g., 1/30s or slower) to blur moving subjects and create dynamic effects. For example, use a slow shutter speed to capture the movement of flowing water or light trails from moving vehicles.

6. Exposure Compensation

- Even though you are controlling the shutter speed, you can still adjust the **exposure compensation** to make the image brighter or darker. This allows you to fine-tune the exposure based on your creative vision or lighting conditions.
- Adjust exposure compensation using the **control dial** or **dedicated exposure compensation button**.

7. Shutter Speed Considerations

- **Motion Blur:** Be aware that slow shutter speeds can result in camera shake, which may cause unwanted blur. To counter this, you can:
    - **Increase ISO:** This helps to maintain a faster shutter speed in low-light conditions.
    - **Use a Tripod:** Stabilizes the camera for long exposures and minimizes camera shake.
- **Fast Shutter Speeds:** Ensure adequate lighting or a higher ISO setting to prevent underexposure.

8. Creative Applications

- **Action Shots:** Use fast shutter speeds to capture sharp images of fast-moving subjects, such as sports or wildlife photography.

- **Long Exposure Photography:** Use slow shutter speeds to capture light trails, create silky smooth water effects, or document motion in a creative way.

- **Night Photography:** Slow shutter speeds combined with a tripod can capture detailed night scenes, such as cityscapes or star trails.

9. Shutter Speed and Lens Performance

- The **Leica DC Vario-Summilux 10.9–34mm f/1.7–2.8 ASPH. lens** allows for a wide range of shutter speeds while maintaining optimal image quality. The wide aperture helps compensate for slower shutter speeds in low-light situations.

Use Cases for Shutter Priority Mode:

- **Sports and Action Photography:** Use fast shutter speeds to freeze motion and capture crisp, clear images of athletes or fast-moving subjects.

- **Creative Motion Effects:** Use slow shutter speeds to introduce intentional blur, such as capturing the movement of flowing water or light trails.

- **Low-Light Photography:** Use slower shutter speeds to allow more light onto the sensor, combined with a tripod to avoid camera shake.

Key Features of Shutter Priority Mode (S):

- **Manual Shutter Speed Control:** Direct control over the shutter speed for creative effects and precise motion capture.

- **Automatic Aperture Adjustment:** The camera automatically selects the appropriate aperture for proper exposure.

- **Exposure Compensation:** Allows fine-tuning of brightness and darkness while maintaining control over shutter speed.

- **Wide Range of Speeds:** From fast to slow, enabling both action shots and long-exposure creativity.

In Shutter Priority Mode, the Leica D-Lux (Typ 109) provides precise control over how motion is captured, whether you want to freeze a fast-moving subject or create dynamic effects with intentional blur. This mode is ideal for both action photography and creative long-exposure shots, offering versatility and flexibility in various shooting scenarios.

Manual Mode (M)

Manual Mode (M) on the Leica D-Lux (Typ 109) gives you full control over both the aperture and shutter speed, allowing for complete creative freedom and precise exposure adjustments. This mode is ideal for photographers who want to fine-tune their settings to achieve specific artistic effects or handle challenging lighting conditions.

1. What is Manual Mode?

- **Manual Mode (M)** allows you to independently set both the **aperture** (f-stop) and the **shutter speed**, without any automatic adjustments from the camera. This gives you complete control over the exposure and depth of field.

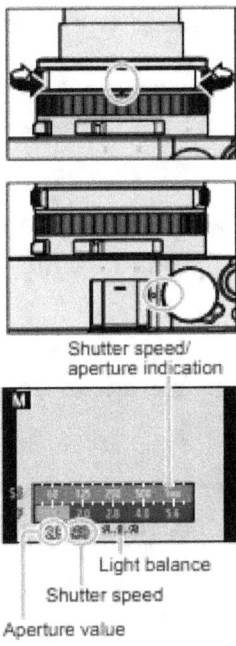

2. How to Use Manual Mode

- **Step 1:** Turn the **mode dial** to **M (Manual Mode)**.
- **Step 2:** Adjust the **aperture** using the **aperture ring** or controls on the camera.
- **Step 3:** Set the **shutter speed** using the **shutter speed dial** or control dial.
- **Step 4:** Check the exposure settings in the camera's display or viewfinder. You can use the **exposure meter** (usually displayed as a scale with a needle or indicator) to gauge if your settings are correct.
- **Step 5:** Compose your shot and adjust the settings as needed to ensure proper exposure.
- **Step 6:** Half-press the **shutter release button** to focus, and then fully press it to capture the image.

3. Exposure Triangle

- The **Exposure Triangle** involves the interplay between **aperture, shutter speed**, and **ISO**. In Manual Mode, you control the first two, and the ISO setting can be adjusted separately to ensure the correct exposure.

- **Aperture:** Controls the amount of light entering the lens and the depth of field.
- **Shutter Speed:** Determines how long the sensor is exposed to light.
- **ISO:** Adjusts the sensor's sensitivity to light. Higher ISO values allow for shooting in lower light but may introduce noise.

4. Exposure Meter

- The camera features an **exposure meter** that helps you achieve proper exposure:
    - **Centre-Weighted Metering:** Measures the light in the centre of the frame and adjusts based on that area.
    - **Evaluative/Matrix Metering:** Measures light across the entire frame and adjusts exposure based on various factors.
    - **Spot Metering:** Measures light in a small area of the frame, which is useful for high-contrast scenes.
- The exposure meter will show whether your settings are overexposed, underexposed, or correctly exposed. Adjust the aperture, shutter speed, or ISO based on this feedback.

5. Creative Control with Manual Mode

- **Depth of Field:** Choose the aperture size to control the depth of field, affecting how much of the image is in focus.
- **Motion Blur:** Select the shutter speed to control motion blur or freeze motion, depending on the speed of the subject and desired effect.
- **Exposure Compensation:** Use the ISO setting to adjust exposure without changing the aperture or shutter speed, helping to handle different lighting conditions.

6. Setting Up Manual Mode

- **Aperture Settings:** Rotate the aperture ring or use the camera's controls to set your desired f-stop. Wider apertures (e.g., f/1.7) let in more light and create a shallow depth of field, while narrower apertures (e.g., f/8) let in less light and increase depth of field.
- **Shutter Speed Settings:** Adjust the shutter speed dial to select the speed at which the shutter opens and closes. Faster speeds (e.g., 1/1000s) are used for freezing motion, while slower speeds (e.g., 1/4s) allow more light and can create motion blur effects.
- **ISO Settings:** Adjust the ISO value to handle different lighting conditions. Lower ISO (e.g., 100) is ideal for bright conditions, while higher ISO (e.g., 3200) is useful in low-light situations but may introduce noise.

7. Common Challenges in Manual Mode

- **Exposure Balance:** Balancing aperture and shutter speed can be tricky. If you change one setting, you may need to adjust the other to maintain proper exposure.
- **Low-Light Situations:** In low light, you may need to use a wider aperture or slower shutter speed. Be cautious of camera shake; using a tripod can help.

- **Motion Blur:** If the shutter speed is too slow, moving subjects may appear blurred. Increase the shutter speed or use stabilization techniques.

8. Practical Applications of Manual Mode

- **Long Exposure Photography:** Capture light trails, star trails, or nighttime landscapes by using long shutter speeds and a stable tripod.
- **Creative Portraits:** Use a wide aperture to create a shallow depth of field and isolate your subject from the background.
- **Action Shots:** Adjust the shutter speed to freeze fast-moving subjects or create motion blur for a dynamic effect.
- **High-Contrast Scenes:** Use Manual Mode to handle challenging lighting conditions, such as bright sunlight with deep shadows or backlit subjects.

Key Features of Manual Mode (M):

- **Full Creative Control:** Adjust both aperture and shutter speed independently for complete creative freedom.
- **Exposure Meter:** Provides feedback on exposure balance to guide your settings.
- **ISO Adjustment:** Separate control of ISO for additional exposure flexibility.
- **Custom Settings:** Fine-tune settings for specific photographic effects and conditions.

In Manual Mode, the Leica D-Lux (Typ 109) empowers you to take full control of your exposure settings, allowing for precise adjustments and creative experimentation. This mode is perfect for photographers who want to master their craft and capture images exactly as they envision them.

Program Mode (P)

Program Mode (P) on the Leica D-Lux (Typ 109) offers a balance between full automation and manual control. In this mode, the camera automatically selects both the aperture and shutter speed for optimal exposure based on the lighting conditions, but you still have the ability to make adjustments and access additional creative features.

1. What is Program Mode?

- **Program Mode (P)** automatically determines the optimal aperture and shutter speed settings for a correct exposure based on the scene's lighting. This allows you to focus on composition and framing while the camera handles the technical aspects of exposure.
- While the camera chooses the settings, you can still adjust other aspects of the shot, such as ISO and exposure compensation.

2. How to Use Program Mode

- **Step 1:** Turn the **mode dial** to **P (Program Mode)**.

- **Step 2:** Compose your shot and let the camera select the appropriate aperture and shutter speed based on the lighting conditions.

- **Step 3:** If desired, adjust the **ISO** setting for different light conditions or use the **exposure compensation** feature to fine-tune the exposure.

- **Step 4:** Half-press the **shutter release button** to focus, and then fully press it to capture the image.

3. Advantages of Using Program Mode

- **Ease of Use:** Ideal for quick shooting and for beginners who want to focus on composition rather than exposure settings.

- **Automatic Adjustments:** The camera automatically calculates exposure settings, making it suitable for dynamic and changing lighting conditions.

- **Creative Flexibility:** While the camera handles the exposure settings, you can still make adjustments such as changing ISO or using exposure compensation to adapt to different scenarios.

4. Exposure Compensation

- **Program Shift:** In Program Mode, you can use **Program Shift** to manually select different combinations of aperture and shutter speed that are still within the camera's recommended exposure range.
    - **How to Use Program Shift:** Rotate the **control dial** or use the **Program Shift feature** to cycle through different exposure combinations without altering the overall exposure.

- **Exposure Compensation:** Adjust the exposure compensation to make the image brighter or darker. This can be done using the **dedicated exposure compensation button** or control dial.

5. ISO Settings

- Adjust the **ISO** setting based on the lighting conditions:
    - **Lower ISO (e.g., 100 or 200):** Best for bright conditions or when using a tripod.
    - **Higher ISO (e.g., 800 or 3200):** Useful for low-light conditions but may introduce noise.

6. Program Mode and Creative Control

- **Program Shift:** Allows you to override the camera's default aperture and shutter speed combinations to achieve specific effects or adapt to different shooting conditions.

- **Custom Settings:** You can still use various shooting modes and features like white balance, focus modes, and more while in Program Mode.

7. Practical Applications

- **Everyday Photography:** Perfect for general shooting where quick adjustments and reliable exposure are needed without manual settings.

- **Travel Photography:** Ideal for capturing moments on the go when you need to quickly adapt to changing lighting conditions.

- **Portraits and Landscapes:** Use Program Shift to adjust depth of field and motion blur while maintaining proper exposure.

Key Features of Program Mode (P):

- **Automatic Exposure:** Camera selects the optimal aperture and shutter speed for proper exposure.

- **Program Shift:** Allows you to manually adjust aperture and shutter speed combinations while maintaining correct exposure.

- **Exposure Compensation:** Enables fine-tuning of exposure to achieve the desired brightness or darkness.

- **ISO Adjustment:** Separate control of ISO for flexibility in different lighting conditions.

In Program Mode, the Leica D-Lux (Typ 109) provides a convenient and efficient way to handle exposure while still offering some creative flexibility. This mode is well-suited for a wide range of shooting situations, allowing you to quickly capture high-quality images without needing to manually adjust every setting

Scene Modes (SCN)

Scene Modes (SCN) on the Leica D-Lux (Typ 109) are pre-set configurations tailored for specific types of photography. Each Scene Mode optimizes the camera's settings to best capture particular scenarios, making it easier to achieve great results without manual adjustments.

1. What are Scene Modes?

- Scene Modes are specialized settings that adjust the camera's aperture, shutter speed, ISO, and other parameters to suit different shooting environments and subjects. They simplify the process of capturing high-quality images in various conditions by automatically selecting the best settings.

2. Accessing Scene Modes

- **Step 1:** Turn the **mode dial** to **SCN** (Scene Mode).

- **Step 2:** Navigate through the available scene modes using the **camera menu** or **control dial**.

- **Step 3:** Select the appropriate scene mode based on your shooting scenario.

- **Step 4:** Compose your shot and capture the image using the **shutter release button**.

3. Available Scene Modes

- **Portrait:** Optimizes settings for capturing people with a focus on skin tones and background blur (shallow depth of field). Ideal for portraits.

- **Landscape:** Enhances the sharpness and depth of field to capture detailed and expansive scenes. Ideal for landscape photography.

- **Macro:** Adjusts settings to focus on close-up subjects with fine details. Ideal for photographing small objects or flowers.

- **Sports:** Uses a fast shutter speed to freeze motion and capture action shots with minimal blur. Ideal for sports or moving subjects.

- **Night Portrait:** Combines a slower shutter speed with flash to capture both the subject and the background in low-light conditions. Ideal for night-time portraiture.

- **Night Scenery:** Optimizes settings for capturing detailed night scenes without flash. Uses longer exposures to capture light and detail in dark environments.

- **Food:** Adjusts settings to enhance colours and textures of food, making it look appetizing. Ideal for food photography.

- **Panorama:** Allows you to capture wide panoramic images by stitching multiple shots together. Ideal for wide landscapes or cityscapes.

4. Advantages of Using Scene Modes

- **Ease of Use:** Simplifies shooting by automatically selecting the best settings for various scenarios, making it ideal for beginners or quick shooting.

- **Optimized Results:** Ensures that you achieve the best possible image quality for specific types of photography without needing in-depth knowledge of camera settings.

- **Time-Saving:** Reduces the time spent adjusting settings manually, allowing you to focus more on composition and capturing the moment.

5. Using Scene Modes Effectively

- **Choose the Right Mode:** Select the scene mode that best matches your shooting scenario to get the most appropriate settings for that situation.

- **Understand Limitations:** While Scene Modes are convenient, they may not always provide the flexibility needed for more complex or creative shots. Consider switching to other modes for more control if needed.

- **Combine with Other Features:** Utilize other camera features such as exposure compensation or white balance adjustments to further fine-tune your images within the selected Scene Mode.

6. Scene Mode Settings

- **Portrait Mode:** Generally uses a wide aperture to create a shallow depth of field, enhancing focus on the subject while blurring the background.

- **Landscape Mode:** Often uses a narrow aperture to achieve a deep depth of field, ensuring that both the foreground and background are in sharp focus.
- **Macro Mode:** Adjusts focus and aperture to capture fine details of close-up subjects.
- **Sports Mode:** Uses a fast shutter speed to minimize motion blur and capture fast-moving subjects with clarity.
- **Night Portrait and Night Scenery Modes:** Employ longer exposures and adjust sensitivity to light to capture detailed images in low-light conditions.

Key Features of Scene Modes (SCN):

- **Pre-set Configurations:** Automatically adjusts settings for specific types of photography.
- **Simplified Shooting:** Makes it easy to achieve high-quality images without manual adjustments.
- **Quick Selection:** Allows rapid adaptation to different shooting scenarios with minimal setup.

In Scene Modes, the Leica D-Lux (Typ 109) offers a range of pre-configured settings designed to help you capture great images across various scenarios. These modes are especially useful for those who prefer a hassle-free approach to photography or need to quickly adapt to different shooting conditions.

Creative Modes

Creative Modes on the Leica D-Lux (Typ 109) offer various artistic effects and enhancements to help you explore different photographic styles and achieve unique looks. These modes allow you to apply creative filters and adjustments to your images, providing additional tools for artistic expression.

1. What are Creative Modes?

- Creative Modes are special settings or filters that modify the appearance of your photos, enabling you to experiment with different visual effects and styles. These modes enhance your creative possibilities by allowing you to apply predefined effects directly in-camera.

2. Accessing Creative Modes

- **Step 1:** Turn the **mode dial** to **Creative Modes** (often accessed via a dedicated button or menu on the camera).
- **Step 2:** Navigate through the available creative modes using the **camera menu** or **control dial**.
- **Step 3:** Select the desired creative mode or effect.
- **Step 4:** Compose your shot and capture the image with the selected effect applied.

3. Available Creative Modes

- **Artistic Effects:** Apply various artistic filters to create unique visual styles, such as:
    - **Black & White:** Converts your images to monochrome with different contrast and grain settings.
    - **Sepia:** Gives your images a warm, vintage look with a sepia tone.
    - **Vivid Colours:** Enhances colour saturation for more vibrant and striking images.
    - **Soft Focus:** Applies a softening effect to create a dreamy, ethereal look.

- **Photo Styles:** Choose from different photo styles to adjust the overall tone and mood of your images:
    - **Standard:** Provides balanced colour and contrast for general shooting.
    - **Landscape:** Enhances colours and sharpness for landscape photography.
    - **Portrait:** Adjusts colour and contrast for flattering skin tones in portrait photography.
    - **Neutral:** Offers a flat colour profile for more flexible post-processing.

- **Creative Filters:** Use filters to add artistic touches or simulate different effects:
    - **Toy Camera:** Adds vignetting and colour shifts for a retro or toy-camera effect.
    - **Dynamic Monochrome:** Provides high-contrast black-and-white images with detailed textures.
    - **Colour Filters:** Apply various colour filters to adjust mood and tone, such as red, green, or blue filters.

4. Advantages of Using Creative Modes

- **Instant Effects:** Apply creative filters and effects in-camera, eliminating the need for post-processing software.
- **Creative Experimentation:** Explore different visual styles and artistic effects to enhance your photography.
- **Time-Saving:** Quickly achieve desired looks without spending time on editing or adjustments in post-production.

5. Using Creative Modes Effectively

- **Experiment:** Try out different creative modes and filters to find the ones that best suit your style and the subject matter.
- **Preview Effects:** Many cameras allow you to preview the effect in real-time on the LCD screen or viewfinder before capturing the image.
- **Combine with Other Settings:** Use creative modes in conjunction with other camera settings, such as exposure compensation or white balance, to fine-tune your images.

6. Creative Mode Settings

- **Artistic Effects:** Adjust settings such as filter intensity or effect strength to achieve the desired look.

- **Photo Styles:** Select the style that best fits the subject and scene to enhance colours, contrast, or tones.

- **Filters:** Choose and adjust filters to create specific effects, such as adding vignetting or changing colour saturation.

Key Features of Creative Modes:

- **Artistic Filters:** Apply predefined effects and styles to create unique and artistic images.

- **Photo Styles:** Adjust colour, contrast, and tone to suit different types of photography.

- **Creative Experimentation:** Provides a range of effects and filters for creative exploration.

- **Instant Application:** Apply effects in-camera for immediate results without post-processing.

In Creative Modes, the Leica D-Lux (Typ 109) offers a range of artistic filters and styles to enhance your photographic creativity. These modes make it easy to experiment with different looks and effects, allowing you to capture images with a unique and personal touch directly in-camera.

CHAPTER SIX
CAMERA OVERVIEW

Autofocus (AF) Settings

The **Leica D-Lux 8** offers a versatile autofocus (AF) system designed to accommodate various shooting scenarios. Here's a detailed overview of its autofocus settings and features:

Autofocus Modes

1. **Intelligent AF**:
   - This mode automatically switches between **AFs** (single autofocus) and **AFc** (continuous autofocus) based on the subject's movement. It is suitable for a wide range of photographic situations.

2. **AFs (Single Autofocus)**:
   - Best for stationary subjects. The camera focuses once when the shutter button is half-pressed, and the focus remains locked as long as the button is held down. This mode is ideal for portraits or landscapes where the subject does not move.

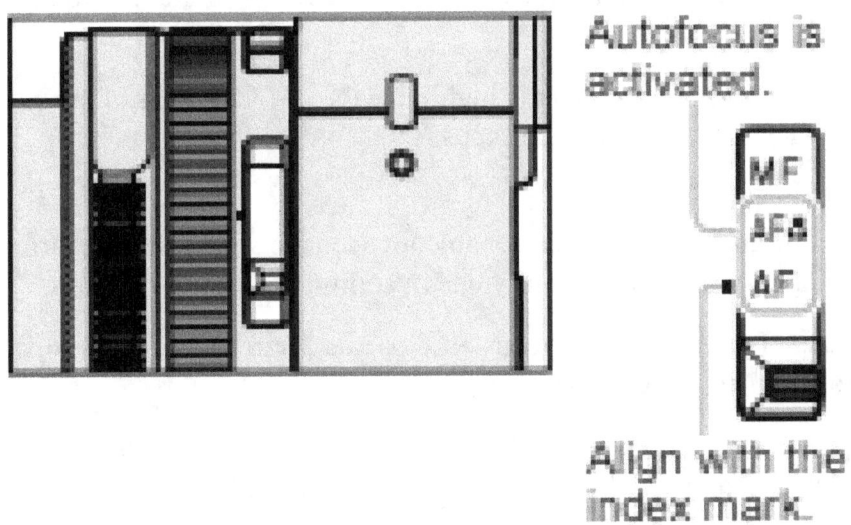

3. **AFc (Continuous Autofocus)**:
   - Designed for moving subjects, this mode continuously adjusts focus as long as the shutter button is pressed halfway. It is useful for capturing action shots or subjects in motion.

Focusing Operation

- **Focus Mode Dial**: The focus mode can be easily switched using the focus mode setting dial on the camera.

- **AF Frame Positioning**: Users can position the AF frame on the desired subject in the viewfinder or LCD screen before taking a shot.
- **Feedback Indicators**:
  - A successful focus is indicated by a **green AF frame**, while an unsuccessful focus attempt is shown with a **red AF frame**.

Metering Methods

The D-Lux 8 offers several metering methods for autofocus:

- **Multi-Field**: The camera evaluates multiple points in the frame to determine the best focus.
- **Single-Field**: Focus is determined from a single point, which can be repositioned by the user.
- **Face Detection**: This feature allows the camera to recognize and focus on human faces, enhancing portrait photography.

Manual Focus (MF)

- The D-Lux 8 also supports manual focusing. Users can switch to **MF mode** using the focus mode dial and then utilize the dedicated focus ring on the lens to achieve precise focus.
- **Focus Peaking**: This feature visually highlights the in-focus areas of the image, making it easier to achieve accurate manual focus.

Additional Features

- **Acoustic Confirmation**: Users can enable an acoustic signal that confirms successful focus metering, providing an auditory cue in addition to visual feedback.
- **Macro Focus**: The camera can focus as close as **3 cm** (1.2 inches) in macro mode, allowing for detailed close-up photography.
- **Continuous Shooting**: The D-Lux 8 supports continuous shooting at up to **11 frames per second** in AF mode, making it suitable for capturing fast-moving subjects.

In summary, the Leica D-Lux 8's autofocus system is designed to be flexible and user-friendly, offering various modes and settings to accommodate different shooting styles and subjects. Whether using automatic focus for dynamic scenes or manual focus for precise control, the D-Lux 8 provides photographers with the tools needed for effective image capture.

Manual Focus (MF) Options

The Leica D-Lux 8 provides several options for manual focusing (MF), allowing photographers to achieve precise control over their focus settings. Here's a detailed overview of the manual focus options available:

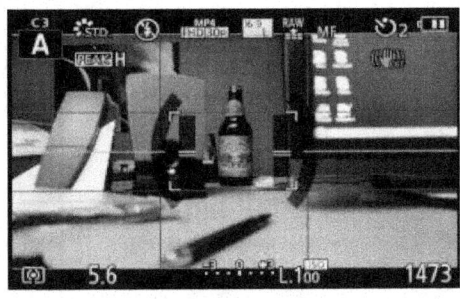
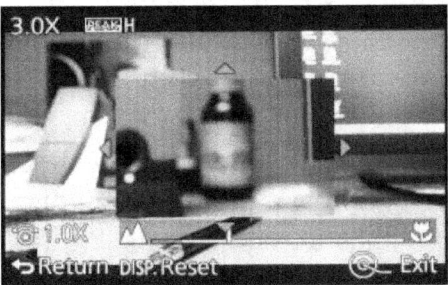

The screen before touching the focusing ring — Clearly out of focus

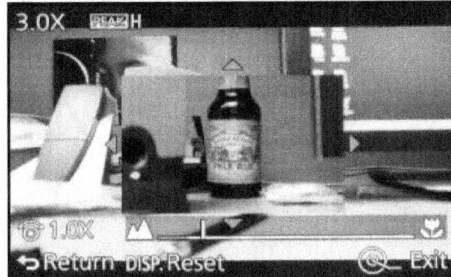
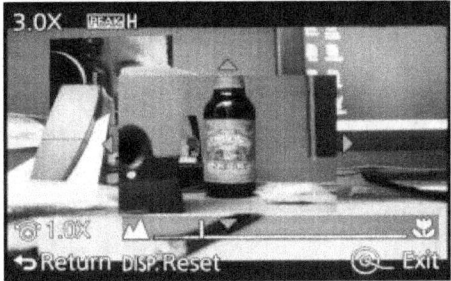

Setting Up Manual Focus

1. **Switch to MF Mode**:

    - To engage manual focus, turn the **focus mode setting dial** on the camera to the **MF position**. This dial is typically located on the lens barrel or the camera body.

2. **Using the Focus Ring**:

    - Once in MF mode, use the **focus ring** located on the lens to manually adjust the focus. The ring provides tactile feedback, allowing for fine adjustments to achieve the desired focus on your subject.

Focus Assistance Features

1. **Focus Peaking**:

    - The D-Lux 8 includes a **focus peaking** feature that highlights the edges of in-focus areas within the frame. This visual aid can be set to different colors (blue, green, red, or white), making it easier to see which parts of the image are sharp.

2. **Magnification**:

    - When you start turning the focus ring, the camera automatically magnifies the view in the electronic viewfinder (EVF) or LCD screen. This magnification can be set to **3x or 6x**, providing a closer view of the subject, which is particularly useful for achieving precise focus in macro photography or detailed shots.

3. **Distance Scale**:

    - The camera displays a **distance scale** in MF mode, indicating the distance at which the lens is focused. This feature helps users understand their focus range and make adjustments accordingly.

Close-Up and Macro Focus
- The D-Lux 8 allows for close focusing capabilities:
    - **Standard Mode**: The lens can focus as close as **19.7 inches** (50 cm).
    - **Macro Mode**: In macro mode, the lens can focus as close as **3 cm** (1.2 inches) at the wide-angle setting, enabling detailed close-up photography of subjects like flowers or small objects.

Additional Considerations
- **Focus Breathing**: The lens optics of the D-Lux 8 exhibit minimal focus breathing, which is advantageous for video recording as it allows for smooth focus transitions without noticeable changes in the angle of view.
- **User Experience**: Many users find the manual focus experience on the D-Lux 8 to be smooth and intuitive, thanks to the well-designed focus ring and the helpful focus assistance features.

In summary, the Leica D-Lux 8 offers a robust manual focus system that enhances creative control for photographers. With features like focus peaking, magnification, and a distance scale, users can achieve precise focus for a variety of shooting scenarios, from portraits to macro photography.

Exposure Compensation

The Leica D-Lux 8 features an effective exposure compensation system that allows photographers to adjust the exposure level to achieve desired results in various lighting conditions. Here are the key details regarding exposure compensation on this camera:

Exposure Compensation Features
1. **Range**: The D-Lux 8 allows for exposure compensation adjustments of **±3 EV** (exposure values). This range enables users to lighten or darken their images effectively.

2. **Increment Settings**: Adjustments can be made in **1/3 EV increments**, providing fine control over exposure settings. This level of precision is helpful for making subtle changes to exposure without drastically altering the image.

3. **Accessing Exposure Compensation**:
    - The camera features a **customizable command dial** that allows quick access to exposure compensation settings. This is an improvement over previous models that had a fixed exposure compensation dial, making it more user-friendly.
    - Users can easily rotate the dial to adjust the exposure compensation while composing their shots.

4. **Automatic Bracketing**: The D-Lux 8 also supports automatic bracketing, allowing users to capture multiple exposures in a single sequence. This feature can be set to take **3, 5, or 7 frames** with graduations between shots of up to **1 EV**, also in **1/3 EV**

increments. This is useful for HDR photography or ensuring that at least one image has the desired exposure.

5. **Real-Time Preview**: The camera provides a live preview of how exposure compensation affects the image on the LCD screen or electronic viewfinder (EVF). This feature allows users to see the impact of their adjustments before taking the shot.

Practical Applications

- **Bright Conditions**: In bright lighting situations, such as sunny days, users may need to dial down the exposure to avoid blown highlights.

- **Low-Light Situations**: Conversely, in low-light conditions, increasing the exposure compensation can help to brighten the image and capture more detail.

- **Creative Control**: Exposure compensation is also a valuable tool for creative photography, allowing users to intentionally overexpose or underexpose images for artistic effects.

In summary, the Leica D-Lux 8's exposure compensation system is designed to provide photographers with flexibility and control over their images, making it easier to adapt to various shooting environments and achieve the desired exposure.

ISO Sensitivity

ISO Sensitivity is a crucial setting on the **Leica D-Lux (Typ 109)** that affects the camera's sensitivity to light, thereby influencing how bright or dark your images appear. Adjusting the ISO setting allows you to optimize your camera's performance in various lighting conditions.

1. What is ISO Sensitivity?

- **ISO Sensitivity** measures the camera sensor's ability to capture light. A higher ISO value increases sensitivity, allowing for better performance in low-light conditions but may introduce more noise (graininess). A lower ISO value reduces sensitivity and is ideal for bright conditions, producing cleaner images with less noise.

2. Adjusting ISO Sensitivity

- **Step 1:** Access the ISO setting through the **camera menu** or by using the **dedicated ISO button** if available.

- **Step 2:** Use the **control dial** or **menu options** to select the desired ISO value.

- **Step 3:** Confirm the setting and exit the menu. The ISO value will be displayed on the LCD screen or viewfinder.

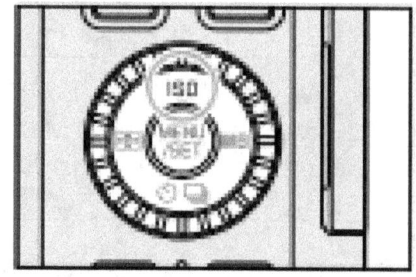

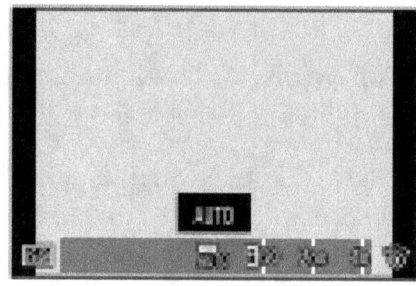

3. ISO Range on Leica D-Lux (Typ 109)

- The Leica D-Lux (Typ 109) typically offers a range of ISO settings, including:
    - **Low ISO (e.g., 100 or 200):** Best for bright conditions or when using a tripod. Provides the cleanest images with minimal noise.
    - **Medium ISO (e.g., 400 to 1600):** Suitable for standard shooting conditions and moderately low light. Balances noise and sensitivity.
    - **High ISO (e.g., 3200 and above):** Useful for low-light situations or when faster shutter speeds are needed. May introduce more noise, which can be managed with noise reduction techniques.

4. When to Adjust ISO Sensitivity

- **Low-Light Conditions:** Increase the ISO to capture images in dim environments without using a flash. This helps maintain faster shutter speeds to reduce motion blur.
- **Bright Conditions:** Use a lower ISO to avoid overexposure and achieve optimal image quality with minimal noise.
- **Fast Motion:** Raise the ISO to allow for faster shutter speeds, helping to freeze fast-moving subjects and reduce motion blur.

5. ISO and Exposure

- **ISO, Aperture, and Shutter Speed:** The ISO setting is part of the exposure triangle, along with aperture and shutter speed. Adjusting ISO changes the sensitivity of the sensor, which can be balanced with adjustments to aperture and shutter speed to achieve proper exposure.
- **Exposure Compensation:** You can use exposure compensation in conjunction with ISO adjustments to fine-tune exposure based on your shooting needs.

6. Noise and Image Quality

- **Noise Reduction:** Higher ISO values can introduce noise (graininess) into images. The Leica D-Lux (Typ 109) typically includes noise reduction features to minimize this effect.

- **Image Quality:** For the best image quality, use the lowest ISO possible for the given lighting conditions. Increase ISO only as needed to maintain proper exposure.

7. Practical Tips for Using ISO Sensitivity

- **Use Auto ISO:** The camera may have an Auto ISO feature that adjusts ISO based on the lighting conditions and shooting mode. This can be useful for quick shooting in varying light.

- **Test Different Settings:** Experiment with different ISO settings to see how they affect image quality and noise levels in various lighting situations.

- **Review Noise Levels:** Check your images at higher ISO settings to ensure noise levels are acceptable for your needs. Adjust ISO and use noise reduction techniques if necessary.

Key Features of ISO Sensitivity:

- **Adjustable Sensitivity:** Control the camera's sensitivity to light with a range of ISO settings.

- **Low and High ISO:** Use lower ISO for bright conditions and higher ISO for low light.

- **Noise Management:** Higher ISO can introduce noise, but noise reduction features can help manage this.

- **Exposure Balance:** ISO is part of the exposure triangle, affecting how aperture and shutter speed work together to achieve proper exposure.

ISO Sensitivity on the Leica D-Lux (Typ 109) allows you to adapt your camera's performance to different lighting conditions, balancing image quality and exposure. By understanding and adjusting ISO, you can enhance your ability to capture clear and well-exposed images in various environments.

Metering Modes

Metering Modes determine how the Leica D-Lux (Typ 109) measures light to calculate the correct exposure for your shots. Different metering modes analyse light in various ways, helping you achieve optimal exposure based on your scene's characteristics. Understanding these modes can significantly impact the quality of your images.

1. What are Metering Modes?

- **Metering Modes** control how the camera evaluates the brightness of the scene to set the appropriate exposure. Each mode uses different areas of the frame or methods to measure light, influencing how exposure settings (aperture, shutter speed, ISO) are determined.

2. Available Metering Modes

- **Evaluative/Matrix Metering:**
  - **Description:** Measures light across the entire frame and evaluates various areas to determine the best overall exposure. It considers factors such as the subject's position, background, and lighting conditions.
  - **Advantages:** Provides balanced exposure for most scenes, making it suitable for general photography.
  - **When to Use:** Ideal for standard shooting situations where you want a well-rounded exposure based on the entire scene.

- **Centre-Weighted Metering:**
  - **Description:** Focuses primarily on the central portion of the frame while still considering the surrounding areas. This mode gives more weight to the central area for exposure calculations.
  - **Advantages:** Useful for situations where the subject is cantered, ensuring that the subject's exposure is accurate even if the background is very bright or dark.
  - **When to Use:** Ideal for portrait photography or when the main subject is in the centre of the frame, and you want to ensure it is properly exposed.

- **Spot Metering:**
  - **Description:** Measures light from a small spot in the centre of the frame (or a selected point) to determine exposure. This mode is very focused and provides exposure based on a specific area.
  - **Advantages:** Allows for precise control over exposure in high-contrast scenes or when you need to expose for a specific part of the image.
  - **When to Use:** Ideal for scenes with significant contrast or when photographing subjects that require precise exposure control, such as in backlit conditions or very detailed close-ups.

3. How to Select and Use Metering Modes

- **Step 1:** Access the metering mode options through the **camera menu** or **settings dial**.
- **Step 2:** Select the desired metering mode based on your shooting scenario.
- **Step 3:** Compose your shot and allow the camera to measure light using the selected metering mode.
- **Step 4:** Review the exposure settings and make any necessary adjustments using ISO, aperture, or shutter speed.

4. When to Use Each Metering Mode

- **Evaluative/Matrix Metering:** Use this mode for most general photography, including landscapes and everyday scenes where you need an overall balanced exposure.

- **Centre-Weighted Metering:** Choose this mode when you want to ensure that the subject in the centre of the frame is correctly exposed, such as in portrait photography or when the background has extreme brightness or darkness.

- **Spot Metering:** Opt for spot metering in high-contrast situations where precise exposure is needed for a specific part of the scene, such as when dealing with strong backlighting or small, detailed subjects.

5. Tips for Effective Metering

- **Check Exposure Preview:** Many cameras provide an exposure preview or histogram to help you evaluate the exposure. Use this to check if your selected metering mode is giving the desired results.

- **Combine with Exposure Compensation:** If the metering mode does not provide the desired exposure, use exposure compensation to adjust brightness.

- **Use Spot Metering Judiciously:** Be cautious with spot metering as it measures only a small area. Ensure that the spot aligns with the key part of your subject for accurate exposure.

Key Features of Metering Modes:

- **Evaluative/Matrix Metering:** Measures light across the entire frame for balanced exposure.

- **Centre-Weighted Metering:** Focuses on the central area of the frame while considering surrounding light.

- **Spot Metering:** Measures light from a specific small area for precise exposure control.

- **Exposure Adjustment:** Allows for tailored exposure settings based on scene characteristics.

Understanding and utilizing the different **Metering Modes** on the Leica D-Lux (Typ 109) can greatly enhance your ability to capture well-exposed images in various lighting conditions. Each mode offers unique advantages for different shooting scenarios, allowing you to achieve optimal results based on your creative vision and the demands of the scene.

CHAPTER SEVEN
WHITE BALANCE AND COLOUR SETTINGS

Auto White Balance

The Leica D-Lux 8 features an advanced Auto White Balance (AWB) system designed to deliver accurate colour reproduction across various lighting conditions. Here's a detailed overview of how the Auto White Balance works and the options available:

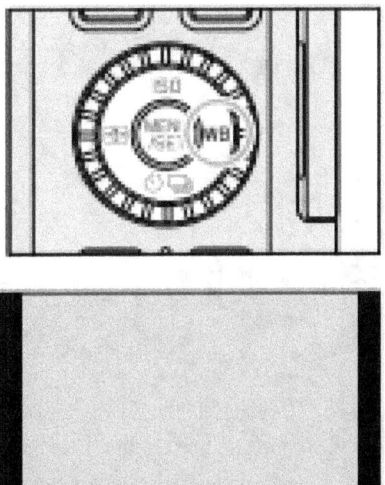

Auto White Balance Overview

1. **Functionality**: The AWB setting automatically adjusts the colour balance of images based on the lighting conditions. This feature is particularly useful for ensuring that whites appear neutral, regardless of the light source, which can vary from natural sunlight to artificial lighting.

2. **Default Setting**: The factory setting for the D-Lux 8 is set to **Auto**, which is suitable for most shooting scenarios. In this mode, the camera analyses the scene and makes real-time adjustments to achieve neutral colour tones.

3. **Fixed Presets**: In addition to the Auto setting, the D-Lux 8 offers several fixed white balance presets that cater to common lighting situations:

   - **Daylight**: For outdoor shooting in sunlight.
   - **Cloudy**: For shooting in overcast conditions.
   - **Shadow**: For subjects in shadowed areas.
   - **Tungsten**: For indoor shooting under incandescent lighting.
   - **Flash**: For use with flash photography.

4. **Manual Settings**: Users can also manually set the white balance using two methods:

- **Gray Card Metering**: This method captures all colour hues in the metering field and calculates a mean gray value. To use this, select the Gray Card option in the menu, aim at a neutral gray or white area, and press the shutter to take a measurement. This setting will remain until a new measurement is taken or a different white balance setting is selected.

- **Direct Colour Temperature Setting**: Users can directly input a colour temperature value ranging from **2500K to 10000K**. This allows for precise control over colour rendering to match specific lighting conditions or personal preferences.

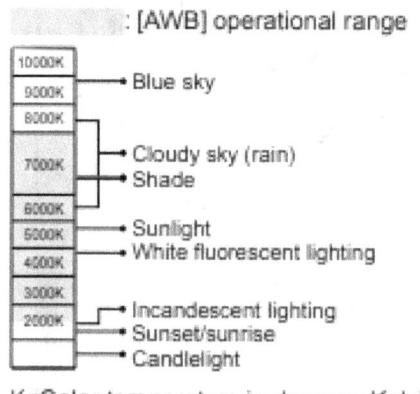

5. **User Experience**: The D-Lux 8's AWB system is designed to deliver neutral results in most situations, making it a reliable choice for both amateur and professional photographers. The camera's ability to adapt to various lighting conditions enhances its versatility, allowing users to focus more on composition rather than technical adjustments.

6. **Live Preview**: The camera provides a live preview of the white balance adjustments on the LCD screen, allowing users to see how changes affect the image in real-time before capturing it.

The Leica D-Lux 8's Auto White Balance system is designed for ease of use and flexibility, offering automatic adjustments as well as manual control options to cater to diverse shooting environments and personal preferences. This feature enhances the overall photographic experience by ensuring accurate colour reproduction in various lighting conditions.

Preset White Balance Options

The Leica D-Lux 8 offers several preset white balance options, allowing users to achieve accurate colour representation under various lighting conditions. Here are the available preset white balance settings:

1. **Auto**: The default setting that automatically adjusts the white balance based on the lighting conditions, delivering neutral results in most situations.

2. **Daylight**: Optimized for shooting in direct sunlight, this setting helps to maintain the natural colour of subjects.

3. **Cloudy**: Designed for overcast or cloudy conditions, this preset adds warmth to the images, counteracting the cool tones often present in such lighting.

4. **Shadow**: This setting is useful for scenes where the subject is in shadow, helping to enhance the colours and reduce the bluish tint that can occur in shaded areas.

5. **Tungsten**: Ideal for indoor shooting under incandescent lighting, this preset compensates for the warm tones of tungsten bulbs, providing a more neutral colon balance.

6. **Flash**: Specifically for use with flash photography, this setting ensures that colours are rendered accurately when using a flash unit.

Additional White Balance Features

- **Manual Metering**: Users can perform manual white balance adjustments using a gray card to achieve precise colour balance based on specific scenes.

- **Colour Temperature Settings**: The D-Lux 8 allows direct setting of colour temperature values ranging from **2500K to 10000K**, providing flexibility for adapting to various light sources and personal preferences.

These preset options, combined with manual adjustments, make the D-Lux 8 versatile for photographers looking to capture accurate colours in different environments

Custom White Balance

The Leica D-Lux 8 allows users to customize white balance settings to achieve precise colour accuracy under different lighting conditions. Here's a detailed explanation of how to set a custom white balance using the camera:

Custom White Balance Setup
Methods for Custom White Balance

1. **Gray Card Metering**:

    - **Purpose**: This method captures all colour hues in the metering field and calculates a mean gray value, providing a tailored white balance for specific lighting conditions.

    - **Procedure**:

        1. **Access the Menu**: Power on the camera and press the **Menu** button.

        2. **Navigate to White Balance**: Scroll through the menu to find the **White Balance** option.

        3. **Select Gray Card**: Choose the **Gray Card** metering option.

        4. **Frame the Gray Card**: Aim the camera at a neutral gray or white area (preferably a gray card) to fill the frame.

5. **Take the Measurement**: Press the shutter button to capture the reference image. The camera will process the information and set the white balance accordingly.
6. **Confirmation**: The custom white balance will remain active until a new measurement is taken or another white balance setting is selected.

2. **Direct Colour Temperature Setting**:
   - **Purpose**: This method allows users to set a specific colour temperature value, providing flexibility for various lighting scenarios.
   - **Procedure**:
     1. **Access the Menu**: Turn on the camera and press the **Menu** button.
     2. **Navigate to White Balance**: Find the **White Balance** section in the menu.
     3. **Select Colour Temperature**: Choose the option for direct colour temperature setting.
     4. **Set the Temperature**: Use the directional pad or touchscreen to select a temperature value between **2500K and 10000K**. This range covers most lighting conditions, from warm indoor lighting to cool daylight.
     5. **Confirm the Setting**: Press the **OK** button to save the selected colour temperature.

Benefits of Custom White Balance
- **Precision**: Custom white balance settings allow photographers to achieve accurate colour reproduction tailored to specific lighting conditions, reducing the need for extensive post-processing.
- **Versatility**: The ability to set both gray card metering and direct colour temperature expands creative options, making the camera adaptable to various environments.
- **Enhanced Control**: Photographers can fine-tune their images to match their artistic vision, ensuring that colours appear as intended in the final photographs.

In summary, the Leica D-Lux 8 provides robust options for setting a custom white balance, enabling users to capture images with accurate colours that reflect the true ambiance of the scene. Whether using gray card metering or directly adjusting colour temperature, these features enhance the overall photographic experience.

Picture Styles

The Leica D-Lux 8 offers a range of picture styles that allow photographers to customize the look and feel of their images. These styles are designed to enhance creativity and provide different aesthetic options for various shooting scenarios. Here's an overview of the available picture styles:

1. **Standard**: This style provides a balanced representation of colours and tones, making it suitable for general photography. It aims to deliver natural-looking images that closely resemble what the eye sees.

2. **Vivid**: The Vivid picture style enhances colour saturation and contrast, resulting in more dynamic and eye-catching images. This style is ideal for landscapes, flowers, and any scene where vibrant colours are desired.

3. **Natural**: Designed to produce softer colours and tones, the Natural style is great for portraits and scenes where a more subdued and realistic representation is preferred.

4. **Monochrome**: This style allows photographers to capture images in black and white, emphasizing textures, shapes, and contrasts without the distraction of colour. It can be further adjusted with filters to simulate classic black-and-white film effects.

5. **Sepia**: The Sepia style gives images a warm, brownish tone reminiscent of vintage photographs. This style is often used for artistic effects or to evoke a sense of nostalgia.

6. **Custom**: Users can create and save their own picture styles by adjusting parameters such as contrast, saturation, and sharpness. This flexibility allows for a personalized approach to image creation.

Additional Features

- **RAW and JPEG Formats**: The D-Lux 8 supports shooting in both RAW (DNG) and JPEG formats. Shooting in RAW allows for greater post-processing flexibility, enabling photographers to fine-tune their images according to their preferred picture style.

- **Aspect Ratio Options**: The camera also allows for multiple aspect ratios (4:3, 3:2, 16:9, and square), which can be combined with different picture styles to achieve unique compositions.

- **Live Preview**: The camera provides a live preview of the selected picture style on the LCD screen, allowing users to see how adjustments will affect the final image before capturing it.

In summary, the Leica D-Lux 8 offers a variety of picture styles that enhance creative expression, allowing photographers to tailor their images to match their artistic vision. Whether aiming for vibrant colours, classic black-and-white, or custom settings, the D-Lux 8 provides the tools needed for versatile photography.

CHAPTER EIGHT
VIDEO RECORDING

Video Resolution and Frame Rates

The **Leica D-Lux (Typ 109)** offers various video recording options to suit different filming needs and preferences. Understanding the available resolutions and frame rates helps you select the best settings for your desired video quality and style.

1. Video Resolutions

- **Full HD (1080p):**
  - **Resolution:** 1920 x 1080 pixels.
  - **Aspect Ratio:** 16:9.
  - **Use:** Provides high-definition video with excellent clarity and detail. Suitable for most standard video needs, including online sharing and playback on HD screens.

- **4K Ultra HD (UHD):**
  - **Resolution:** 3840 x 2160 pixels.
  - **Aspect Ratio:** 16:9.
  - **Use:** Offers four times the resolution of Full HD, providing even greater detail and clarity. Ideal for high-quality video production, detailed scenes, and future-proofing content for higher-resolution displays.

2. Frame Rates

- **24 fps (Frames Per Second):**
  - **Use:** Commonly used in cinema and for achieving a film-like look. Provides a slightly softer motion blur that many viewers associate with movie footage.

- **30 fps:**
  - **Use:** Standard frame rate for television and online video. Provides smoother motion compared to 24 fps and is ideal for general video recording, including vlogs and live streaming.

- **60 fps:**
  - **Use:** Captures more frames per second for smoother motion, especially useful for action shots or fast-moving subjects. It also allows for slow-motion playback if needed.

3. How to Select Video Resolution and Frame Rate

- **Step 1:** Access the video recording settings through the **camera menu**.
- **Step 2:** Select the desired video resolution (e.g., Full HD or 4K).
- **Step 3:** Choose the appropriate frame rate (e.g., 24 fps, 30 fps, or 60 fps) based on your filming needs.
- **Step 4:** Confirm your settings and exit the menu. Your video recording will use the selected resolution and frame rate.

4. Practical Considerations

- **Storage Space:** Higher resolutions and frame rates require more storage space. Ensure you have enough memory card capacity for your chosen settings.
- **Processing Power:** Higher resolution and frame rates demand more processing power from the camera. Ensure your camera is set up to handle the chosen settings efficiently.
- **Editing and Playback:** Consider your final output needs. For example, 4K footage is ideal for high-resolution editing and playback, while Full HD is often sufficient for web content and general viewing.

5. Applications of Different Settings

- **Full HD (1080p) at 30 fps:** Ideal for standard video projects, vlogs, and general content creation. Balances quality and file size.
- **4K UHD at 30 fps or 60 fps:** Perfect for high-quality video production, professional content, and detailed scenes. Provides greater detail and flexibility in post-production, such as cropping or stabilizing footage.
- **Slow Motion:** Using a higher frame rate like 60 fps allows for slow-motion effects when played back at a standard frame rate (e.g., 30 fps).

Key Features of Video Resolution and Frame Rates:

- **Full HD (1080p):** Standard high-definition resolution for clear and detailed video.
- **4K Ultra HD (UHD):** High-resolution option for enhanced detail and future-proofing.
- **24 fps:** Cinematic look with classic film motion blur.
- **30 fps:** Standard frame rate for smooth video and general use.
- **60 fps:** Provides ultra-smooth motion and slow-motion capability.

Understanding the **Video Resolution and Frame Rates** available on the Leica D-Lux (Typ 109) allows you to tailor your video recordings to suit your specific needs and preferences, ensuring high-quality results for various filming scenarios

Recording Videos

Recording videos with the **Leica D-Lux (Typ 109)** involves selecting the appropriate settings and using the camera's controls to capture high-quality video footage. Here's a step-by-step guide to help you get the best results from your video recordings:

1. Preparing for Video Recording

- **Ensure Proper Settings:** Before starting, check that your camera settings are configured for video recording. This includes resolution, frame rate, and any other video-specific settings you might want to adjust.

- **Check Battery and Storage:** Make sure you have a fully charged battery and sufficient memory card space for the duration of your recording.

2. Selecting Video Settings

- **Resolution and Frame Rate:**
    - Access the video settings through the **camera menu**.
    - Choose the desired **resolution** (e.g., Full HD 1080p or 4K UHD) and **frame rate** (e.g., 24 fps, 30 fps, 60 fps) based on your recording needs.

- **Other Settings:**
    - Adjust **focus mode** (e.g., manual or automatic) based on how you want the camera to handle focusing during recording.
    - Set **exposure settings** if needed, such as aperture, shutter speed, and ISO. Consider using manual mode for more control.

3. Starting Video Recording

- **Activate Video Mode:**
    - Turn the **mode dial** to the video recording mode or press the **dedicated video recording button** if available.

- **Compose Your Shot:**
    - Use the **LCD screen** or **viewfinder** to frame your shot and ensure the subject is properly composed.

- **Start Recording:**
    - Press the **shutter release button** or the **dedicated video recording button** to begin recording. The camera will start capturing video based on your selected settings.

- **Monitor Recording:**
    - Keep an eye on the **LCD screen** to monitor the recording process. Ensure that the video is being captured correctly and that there are no issues with focus or exposure.

4. During Recording

- **Adjustments:**
    - Make real-time adjustments as needed, such as zooming in or out, changing focus, or adjusting exposure settings.

- **Stabilization:**
    - If possible, use a tripod or stabilizer to minimize camera shake and ensure smooth footage.

- **Audio:**
    - Ensure that any audio you want to capture is clear. The camera's built-in microphone will record sound, but you might consider an external microphone for higher audio quality.

5. Stopping Video Recording

- **End Recording:**
    - Press the **shutter release button** or **video recording button** again to stop recording. The camera will finalize the video file and save it to the memory card.

- **Review Footage:**
    - Playback the recorded video on the **LCD screen** to ensure it meets your expectations. Check for proper exposure, focus, and audio quality.

6. Post-Recording

- **Transfer Files:**
    - Connect the camera to a computer or use a card reader to transfer the video files from the memory card for editing or sharing.

- **Editing:**
    - Use video editing software to cut, trim, or enhance your footage as needed. You can also adjust colour, add effects, or synchronize audio tracks.

Key Features for Video Recording:

- **Resolution and Frame Rate:** Choose based on the desired video quality and style.
- **Stabilization:** Use a tripod or stabilizer to reduce camera shake.
- **Audio:** Monitor and ensure clear audio capture.
- **Monitoring:** Use the LCD screen or viewfinder to check framing and recording status.

By following these steps and utilizing the features of the Leica D-Lux (Typ 109), you can effectively record high-quality videos tailored to your specific needs and creative vision.

Audio Settings

Audio Settings on the **Leica D-Lux (Typ 109)** allow you to manage how sound is recorded during video capture. While the camera offers basic audio controls, understanding and optimizing these settings can enhance the audio quality of your recordings. Here's an overview of the available audio settings and how to use them effectively:

1. Accessing Audio Settings

- **Step 1:** Go to the **camera menu** by pressing the **Menu** button.
- **Step 2:** Navigate to the **Audio Settings** or **Video Settings** section within the menu.
- **Step 3:** Adjust the available audio settings based on your needs.

2. Microphone Settings

- **Built-in Microphone:** The Leica D-Lux (Typ 109) features a built-in microphone that captures ambient sound during video recording.
    - **Volume Control:** Some cameras allow you to adjust the microphone sensitivity to manage how loudly sounds are captured. If available, set the sensitivity based on the recording environment to avoid distortion or low audio levels.
    - **Wind Noise Reduction:** If the camera has an option for wind noise reduction, enable it to minimize wind interference when recording outdoors.

3. External Microphone (If Supported)

- **Microphone Input:** Check if the camera supports an external microphone via a dedicated input or adapter.
    - **Connection:** Connect an external microphone for higher audio quality. This can be useful for capturing clearer audio, especially in noisy environments or for professional recordings.
    - **Settings Adjustment:** Some cameras allow you to adjust settings for an external microphone, such as input level or gain. Configure these settings to suit the microphone and recording conditions.

4. Audio Levels and Monitoring

- **Audio Levels:** Monitor and adjust audio levels if the camera provides real-time audio level meters or indicators.
    - **Adjust Levels:** Ensure audio levels are set appropriately to avoid clipping (distortion from high levels) or recording too quietly.
- **Monitoring:** If possible, use headphones to monitor audio while recording. This helps ensure that the audio is being captured clearly and allows you to address any issues in real-time.

5. Audio Recording Settings

- **Recording Quality:** Some cameras offer settings for audio recording quality, such as different bit rates or sample rates.
  - **Quality Settings:** Choose the highest quality available for the best audio fidelity. Higher bit rates and sample rates provide better sound quality but may increase file sizes.

6. Post-Processing and Editing

- **Editing Software:** After recording, use audio editing software to clean up and enhance your audio. This may include removing background noise, adjusting levels, or synchronizing audio with video.
- **Synchronization:** Ensure that audio is synchronized with video, especially if using an external microphone or recording audio separately.

Key Audio Settings Features:

- **Built-in Microphone:** Captures ambient sound; adjust sensitivity if possible.
- **External Microphone:** Connect for improved audio quality; configure settings if supported.
- **Audio Levels:** Monitor and adjust to prevent distortion or low levels.
- **Recording Quality:** Choose the highest quality settings available for optimal audio.

By understanding and optimizing the **Audio Settings** on your Leica D-Lux (Typ 109), you can ensure high-quality sound for your video recordings, enhancing the overall production value and clarity of your content.

Playback of Recorded Videos

Playback of recorded videos on the **Leica D-Lux (Typ 109)** allows you to review your footage directly on the camera before transferring it to a computer or other devices. Here's a guide on how to effectively play back and manage your recorded videos:

1. Accessing Playback Mode

- **Step 1:** Turn on the camera and ensure you're in **Playback Mode**.
  - You can usually access Playback Mode by pressing the **Playback button** (often marked with a play icon) on the camera body.
- **Step 2:** If the camera is not in Playback Mode, press the **Playback button** or turn the mode dial to the Playback setting.

2. **Navigating Videos**

    - **Viewing Thumbnails:**

        o The camera may display video thumbnails or a grid view. Use the **arrow keys** or **control dial** to navigate through the available videos.

    - **Selecting a Video:**

        o Highlight the video you want to view and press the **OK** button or **Enter** button to select it.

3. **Playing Videos**

    - **Playback Controls:**

        o Use the **play button** to start video playback. Playback controls typically include:

            - **Play/Pause:** To start or pause playback.
            - **Stop:** To stop playback and return to the video selection screen.
            - **Rewind/Fast Forward:** To navigate through the video quickly.
            - **Skip:** To move to the previous or next video.

    - **Volume Control:**

        o Adjust the volume if the camera provides audio controls during playback. Some cameras have a volume adjustment feature in the playback menu or via physical buttons.

4. **Reviewing Video Information**

    - **Video Details:**

        o While playing a video, you may be able to access additional information such as duration, file size, and recording settings. This information can usually be accessed through a menu or information button.

    - **Playback Quality:**

        o The quality of playback on the camera may differ from what is seen on a larger screen. Ensure the video plays smoothly and is of acceptable quality.

5. **Editing and Deleting Videos**

    - **Basic Editing:**

        o Some cameras offer basic editing functions like trimming or cutting videos directly on the camera. Access these features through the Playback or Editing menu.

    - **Deleting Videos:**

- If you need to delete a video, select it in Playback Mode and choose the delete option. Confirm the deletion when prompted to remove the video from the memory card.

6. Transferring Videos

- **Transfer Options:**
    - For more detailed review and editing, transfer your videos to a computer or other device. Connect the camera to your computer using a USB cable or remove the memory card and use a card reader.

- **File Management:**
    - Use file management software or your computer's file explorer to copy or move videos to your desired location. Ensure the files are backed up and properly organized for further editing or sharing.

7. Playback Tips

- **Check Compatibility:** Ensure that the video format is compatible with your playback device or software.

- **Monitor Quality:** If the video quality is not as expected, check your recording settings and consider adjusting resolution or frame rate for better results in future recordings.

- **Backup Files:** Regularly back up your video files to avoid data loss and ensure you have multiple copies of important footage.

Key Playback Features:

- **Playback Button:** Access video playback mode and controls.
- **Navigation:** Use arrow keys or control dial to select and play videos.
- **Volume Control:** Adjust sound levels during playback.
- **Editing and Deleting:** Basic editing and deletion options available.
- **Transfer:** Move videos to a computer for detailed review and editing.

Using these features, you can effectively review and manage your recorded videos directly on the Leica D-Lux (Typ 109), ensuring you capture and preserve high-quality footage for your projects.

CHAPTER NINE
FLASH PHOTOGRAPHY

Built-in Flash Settings

The **Leica D-Lux (Typ 109)** features a built-in flash that can enhance your photography in low-light conditions or add creative effects to your images. Understanding and utilizing the built-in flash settings can help you achieve better results. Here's a guide to the flash settings and how to use them effectively:

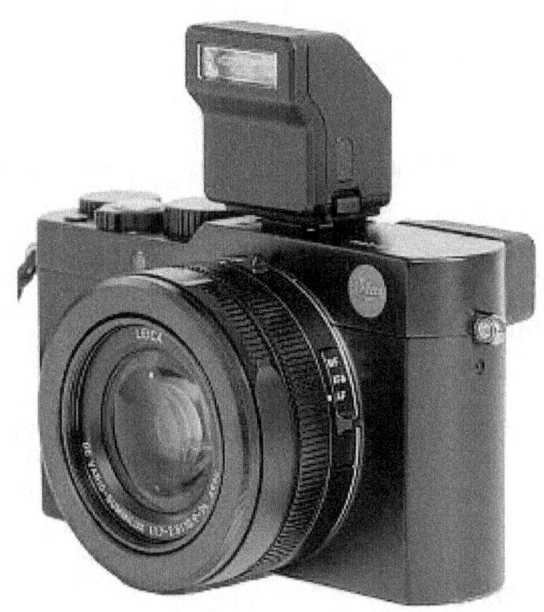

1. Accessing Flash Settings

- **Step 1:** Turn on the camera and set it to **photo mode**.
- **Step 2:** Access the **flash settings** through the **camera menu** or use the dedicated **flash button** if available.
- **Step 3:** Navigate to the **flash settings** option to adjust the flash mode and other related settings.

2. Flash Modes

- **Auto Flash:**
  - **Description:** The camera automatically determines when to use the flash based on the lighting conditions of the scene.
  - **Use:** Ideal for general shooting where you want the camera to handle flash usage automatically.
- **Fill Flash:**
  - **Description:** The flash fires with every shot, regardless of the ambient light. This mode is used to illuminate shadows and balance exposure.

- o **Use:** Useful in bright conditions or to fill in shadows on subjects, especially in backlit situations.

- **Slow Sync Flash:**
  - o **Description:** The flash fires at a slower shutter speed, allowing more ambient light to be captured along with the flash.
  - o **Use:** Ideal for low-light environments where you want to capture both the subject with flash and the background with ambient light. This mode often results in well-lit subjects and more natural-looking backgrounds.

- **Off:**
  - o **Description:** The flash is disabled and will not fire regardless of the lighting conditions.
  - o **Use:** Suitable for situations where flash is not desired or when shooting in well-lit environments.

3. Adjusting Flash Power

- **Flash Compensation:** Some cameras allow you to adjust the flash intensity to increase or decrease its output.
  - o **Access:** Go to the **flash compensation** setting in the menu.
  - o **Adjust:** Increase or decrease the flash power based on your needs to achieve the desired lighting effect.

4. Using the Flash Effectively

- **Distance and Coverage:**
  - o Ensure the subject is within the effective range of the built-in flash. Check the camera's manual for the maximum effective flash range.

- **Avoiding Red-Eye:**
  - o To minimize red-eye, try using red-eye reduction mode if available, or have subjects look away from the lens.

- **Bounce Flash:**
  - o While the built-in flash on the Leica D-Lux (Typ 109) may not support bounce techniques directly, you can use external diffusers or reflectors to soften the light and reduce harsh shadows.

5. Troubleshooting Flash Issues

- **Flash Not Firing:**
  - o Ensure that the flash mode is set correctly and that the flash is not disabled.

- **Insufficient Light:**
    - If images are underexposed, check if the flash mode is appropriate for the scene and adjust the flash compensation if needed.
- **Overexposure:**
    - If images are overexposed, reduce the flash compensation or use a different flash mode to balance the exposure.

Key Flash Settings Features:

- **Auto Flash:** Automatically determines flash usage.
- **Fill Flash:** Fires flash with every shot to fill shadows.
- **Slow Sync Flash:** Combines flash with ambient light for balanced exposure.
- **Off:** Disables the flash.
- **Flash Compensation:** Adjusts flash intensity for better exposure control.

By utilizing the **built-in flash settings** effectively, you can enhance your photography in various lighting conditions and achieve well-exposed, balanced images with the Leica D-Lux (Typ 109).

Flash Modes

The Leica D-Lux (Typ 109) offers various flash modes to help you achieve the desired lighting effects for your photographs. Here's a detailed overview of the available flash modes and how to use them:

1. Auto Flash

- **Description:** The camera automatically decides when to use the flash based on the lighting conditions of the scene. It assesses the ambient light and determines if the flash is needed to properly expose the image.
- **Use:** Ideal for everyday shooting where you want the camera to handle flash usage without manual intervention. Useful for general situations where you need a bit of extra light to enhance your photo.

2. Fill Flash

- **Description:** The flash fires with every shot, regardless of the ambient light. This mode is used to illuminate the subject even in well-lit conditions or to balance exposure between the subject and background.
- **Use:** Useful in bright conditions, such as outdoor photography with strong sunlight, where you want to reduce harsh shadows on the subject's face or add light to a subject in a backlit scene.

3. **Slow Sync Flash**

    - **Description:** The flash fires at a slower shutter speed, allowing more ambient light to be captured along with the flash. This mode combines the light from the flash with the existing light in the environment.
    - **Use:** Ideal for low-light or night-time photography where you want to capture both the subject illuminated by the flash and the background with ambient light. This mode helps create images with balanced lighting and more natural-looking backgrounds.

4. **Rear Curtain Sync (If Available)**

    - **Description:** The flash fires at the end of the exposure, just before the shutter closes. This mode captures motion blur behind the subject while using the flash to freeze the subject at the end of the exposure.
    - **Use:** Useful for capturing motion effects with a flash, such as moving subjects with a trailing light effect. This mode is commonly used in creative photography to show motion while keeping the subject well-lit.

5. **Flash Off**

    - **Description:** The flash is disabled and will not fire regardless of the lighting conditions. This mode ensures that no flash light is used in your photography.
    - **Use:** Suitable for situations where you prefer natural lighting or when shooting in well-lit environments where additional flash is unnecessary or undesirable.

How to Access and Use Flash Modes

1. **Access Flash Menu:**

    - Press the **flash button** on the camera body or navigate to the **flash settings** in the camera menu.

2. **Select Flash Mode:**

    - Choose the desired flash mode (e.g., Auto Flash, Fill Flash, Slow Sync Flash) using the camera's control dial or menu options.

3. **Adjust Settings:**

    - If necessary, adjust additional settings such as **flash compensation** to control the intensity of the flash output.

4. **Take Photos:**

    - Compose your shot and press the shutter button. The camera will use the selected flash mode to enhance the lighting of the photograph.

Tips for Using Flash Modes

- **Avoiding Red-Eye:** Use red-eye reduction mode if available, or have subjects look away from the lens to minimize red-eye effects.

- **Balancing Light:** Use Slow Sync Flash to achieve a natural look by combining flash with ambient light, which can enhance the overall quality of your photos in low-light situations.
- **Creative Effects:** Experiment with Rear Curtain Sync (if available) for dynamic shots showing motion blur with a well-lit subject.

Understanding and utilizing the **flash modes** on the Leica D-Lux (Typ 109) allows you to adapt to different lighting conditions and achieve well-exposed, creative photographs.

External Flash Compatibility

The Leica D-Lux (Typ 109) is equipped with a built-in flash, but it does not have a dedicated hot shoe for mounting external flash units. As a result, it does not natively support the attachment of external flash units directly onto the camera body.

1. Limitations

- **No Hot Shoe:** The Leica D-Lux (Typ 109) lacks a hot shoe, which means you cannot attach external flash units that require this mount.
- **No External Flash Ports:** The camera does not have external flash ports or connections for direct integration with external lighting equipment.

2. Alternative Solutions

- **Use Built-In Flash:** Rely on the camera's built-in flash for most lighting needs. The built-in flash offers several modes, including Auto, Fill Flash, and Slow Sync Flash, which can cover various scenarios.
- **External Lighting:** For more advanced lighting needs, consider using external lighting sources that do not require camera mounting, such as:
    - **Off-Camera Flash:** Place an external flash off-camera and use wireless triggers or manual setups to light your subject.
    - **Continuous Lights:** Use continuous lighting sources like LED panels or studio lights for controlled and adjustable lighting conditions.

3. Using Wireless Flash Triggers

- **Wireless Flash Systems:** Some external flashes come with wireless triggers or can be used with remote triggers to fire the flash from a distance. Set up the flash on a stand or in the desired position and use a wireless trigger to activate it.
- **Manual Settings:** Since the camera cannot control the external flash directly, set the external flash to manual mode and adjust the power output to suit your needs. Use trial and error to achieve the desired exposure.

4. Creative Lighting Techniques

- **Bounce Flash:** If using external flash units indirectly, you can bounce the light off surfaces like walls or ceilings to achieve softer, more diffused lighting.

- **Diffusers and Modifiers:** Use diffusers, softboxes, or other light modifiers with external flashes to control and shape the light for better results.

The **Leica D-Lux (Typ 109)** does not support external flash units directly due to the lack of a hot shoe or external flash ports. Users needing advanced lighting setups should rely on the built-in flash for basic needs or explore alternative lighting solutions such as wireless triggers, continuous lights, or off-camera flash setups.

CHAPTER TEN
WIFI AND CONNECTIVITY

Enabling Wi-Fi

The Leica D-Lux (Typ 109) features built-in Wi-Fi, allowing you to connect the camera to your smartphone or tablet for remote control and easy file transfer. Here's how to enable and use the Wi-Fi function on your camera:

1. Accessing Wi-Fi Settings

- **Step 1:** Turn on the camera and ensure it is in **Photo Mode** or any other mode that allows access to the menu.
- **Step 2:** Press the **Menu** button to access the camera's main menu.

2. Enabling Wi-Fi

- **Step 1:** Navigate to the **Wi-Fi Settings** or **Network Settings** in the camera menu.
- **Step 2:** Select **Wi-Fi** or **Wireless** to access the Wi-Fi settings.
- **Step 3:** Turn on Wi-Fi by selecting **Enable** or similar options. The camera will start searching for available networks.

3. Connecting to a Network

- **Step 1:** If you want to connect the camera to a Wi-Fi network (e.g., home network), select the network from the list of available networks.
- **Step 2:** Enter the Wi-Fi password if prompted and connect to the network.

4. Connecting to a Smartphone or Tablet

- **Step 1:** On your smartphone or tablet, download and install the **Leica FOTOS** app from the App Store or Google Play Store.
- **Step 2:** Open the **Leica FOTOS** app and follow the on-screen instructions to connect to your camera. The app may prompt you to connect to the camera's Wi-Fi network.
- **Step 3:** On the camera, select the option to connect to a smartphone or tablet. This may involve selecting **Pairing** or **Connecting to Device** in the Wi-Fi settings.
- **Step 4:** The camera will display a Wi-Fi network name (SSID) and password. Use these details to connect your smartphone or tablet to the camera's Wi-Fi network.
- **Step 5:** Once connected, the app will recognize the camera, and you can begin using remote control features and transferring files.

5. Using Wi-Fi Features

- **Remote Control:** Use the **Leica FOTOS** app to remotely control the camera, including taking photos, adjusting settings, and viewing live previews.

- **File Transfer:** Transfer photos and videos from the camera to your smartphone or tablet for easy sharing and editing.
- **Firmware Updates:** Some camera apps allow you to check for and install firmware updates through the app.

6. Disconnecting Wi-Fi

- **Step 1:** To disconnect the Wi-Fi connection, return to the **Wi-Fi Settings** in the camera menu.
- **Step 2:** Select **Disable** or turn off the Wi-Fi function to disconnect from the network or paired devices.

Troubleshooting Tips

- **Ensure Compatibility:** Make sure your smartphone or tablet is compatible with the Leica FOTOS app.
- **Check Signal Strength:** Ensure that the camera and your device are within range of the Wi-Fi signal.
- **Update App:** Ensure that the Leica FOTOS app is up to date for the best performance and compatibility.
- **Restart Devices:** If you encounter issues, try restarting both the camera and your smartphone or tablet.

Enabling Wi-Fi on the **Leica D-Lux (Typ 109)** allows you to connect the camera to your smartphone or tablet for remote control and file transfer. Follow the steps above to access the Wi-Fi settings, connect to a network or device, and use the available Wi-Fi features to enhance your photography experience.

Connecting to Smart Devices

Connecting the Leica D-Lux 8 to smart devices is straightforward, primarily facilitated through the Leica FOTOS app. Here's how to set up the connection and utilize its features:

Connecting to Smart Devices

1. Download the Leica FOTOS App

- **Availability**: The Leica FOTOS app is available for download from the **Apple App Store** or **Google Play Store**.
- **Compatibility**: Ensure your smartphone or tablet is compatible with the app.

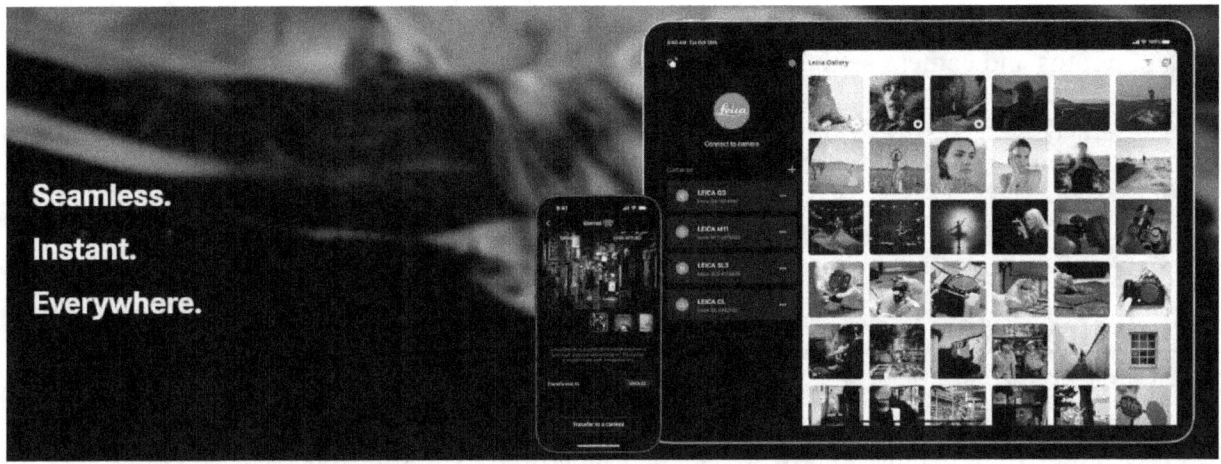

2. **Enable Wi-Fi on the D-Lux 8**

    - **Access the Menu**: Turn on the camera and navigate to the **Menu**.

    - **Select Wi-Fi Settings**: Find the **Wi-Fi** option and enable it. The camera will create a Wi-Fi hotspot.

3. **Connect Your Smart Device**

    - **Wi-Fi Connection**: On your smartphone or tablet, go to the Wi-Fi settings and connect to the network created by the D-Lux 8. The network name will typically include "Leica D-Lux 8."

    - **Password Entry**: If prompted, enter the password displayed on the camera screen.

4. **Open the Leica FOTOS App**

    - **Launch the App**: Once connected, open the Leica FOTOS app on your smart device.

    - **Camera Detection**: The app should automatically detect the D-Lux 8. Follow any on-screen prompts to establish a connection.

5. **Using the App**

    - **Image Transfer**: You can browse and select images from the camera to download directly to your smart device. This includes both JPEG and DNG files.

    - **Remote Control**: The app allows for remote camera operation, including controlling the shutter, adjusting settings, and using the optical zoom.

    - **Editing and Sharing**: Edit photos within the app and share them directly to social media or other platforms.

    - **Firmware Updates**: The app can also be used to check for and install firmware updates for the camera.

Additional Features

- **Geotagging**: The app supports geotagging, allowing you to add location data to your images, which is stored in the EXIF metadata.

- **User-Friendly Interface**: The app provides an intuitive interface for managing your photos and camera settings.

By following these steps, you can seamlessly connect your Leica D-Lux 8 to smart devices, enhancing your photography experience through easy image transfer and remote control capabilities.

Using the Leica Image Shuttle App

The Leica Image Shuttle App is designed to work with various Leica cameras, including the Leica D-Lux (Typ 109), allowing you to control the camera remotely, transfer files, and more. Here's a step-by-step guide on how to use the Leica Image Shuttle App effectively:

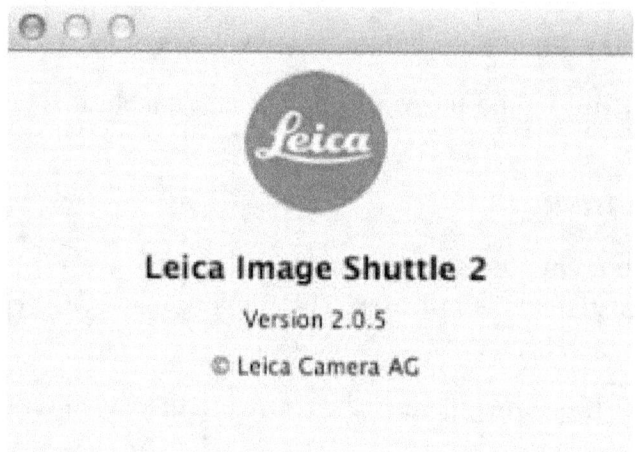

1. Downloading and Installing the App

- **Step 1:** Download the **Leica Image Shuttle App** from the App Store (for iOS devices) or Google Play Store (for Android devices).
- **Step 2:** Install the app on your smartphone or tablet by following the on-screen instructions.

2. Connecting Your Camera to the App

- **Step 1:** Turn on the **Leica D-Lux (Typ 109)** and enable the **Wi-Fi** function. Access the Wi-Fi settings on the camera and select **Enable**.
- **Step 2:** On the camera, choose the option to connect to a smartphone or tablet. You may need to select **Pairing** or **Connect Device** from the Wi-Fi settings menu.
- **Step 3:** Open the **Leica Image Shuttle App** on your smartphone or tablet.
- **Step 4:** The app will prompt you to connect to the camera's Wi-Fi network. Go to your device's Wi-Fi settings and connect to the camera's Wi-Fi network (SSID and password are typically displayed on the camera screen).
- **Step 5:** Once connected, the app will recognize the camera, and you can begin using the app's features.

3. Remote Control Features

- **Live View:** Use the app to view a live preview from the camera's lens. This allows you to frame and compose shots remotely.

- **Camera Settings:** Adjust camera settings such as exposure, aperture, ISO, and focus directly from the app.

- **Capture Photos:** Take photos remotely by using the app's shutter control. This is useful for group shots, long exposures, or when the camera is mounted on a tripod.

4. Transferring Files

- **Select Files:** Use the app to browse the camera's gallery and select the photos or videos you want to transfer.

- **Transfer:** Initiate the transfer process to send selected files to your smartphone or tablet. This allows for quick sharing and editing.

- **Organize:** Once transferred, organize your files on your device using the app's or your device's file management tools.

5. Firmware Updates

- **Check for Updates:** The app may offer the option to check for and install firmware updates for your camera.

- **Install Updates:** Follow the app's instructions to update the camera's firmware, ensuring you have the latest features and improvements.

6. Troubleshooting Tips

- **Ensure Compatibility:** Verify that your smartphone or tablet is compatible with the Leica Image Shuttle App.

- **Check Connection:** Ensure the camera and your device are properly connected to the Wi-Fi network. Restart both devices if you encounter connection issues.

- **Update the App:** Keep the app updated to the latest version for optimal performance and compatibility.

- **App Permissions:** Ensure the app has the necessary permissions to access and transfer files.

The Leica Image Shuttle App allows you to control your Leica D-Lux (Typ 109) remotely, view live previews, adjust settings, and transfer files. By following the steps above, you can leverage the app's features to enhance your photography experience and streamline your workflow.

Transferring Photos to a Computer

Transferring photos from the Leica D-Lux 8 to a computer can be done through several methods, providing flexibility based on your preferences. Here's a breakdown of the available options:

1. **Using a USB Cable**

   - **Connect the Camera**: Use a USB-C cable to connect the D-Lux 8 directly to your computer.

   - **Mass Storage Mode**: The camera can be recognized as a mass storage device, allowing you to browse and transfer files directly from the camera's memory card to your computer.

   - **File Transfer**: Simply drag and drop the desired photos from the camera's storage to your computer.

2. **Using a Memory Card Reader**

   - **Remove the Memory Card**: Take the SD card from the D-Lux 8 and insert it into a compatible SD card reader connected to your computer.

   - **Access Files**: Open the card in your file explorer and copy the photos (in JPEG or DNG format) to your computer.

3. **Leica FOTOS App**

   - **Wireless Transfer**: The D-Lux 8 is compatible with the **Leica FOTOS app**, which allows for wireless transfer of images and videos to your smartphone or tablet.

   - **Setup**: Connect your camera to the app via Wi-Fi. You can then select photos to transfer directly to your mobile device.

   - **Editing and Sharing**: The app also provides options for basic editing and direct sharing to social media platforms.

4. **Direct Upload from Camera**

   - **Using Wi-Fi**: If you prefer not to use cables, you can utilize the built-in Wi-Fi feature to transfer images to a computer that is connected to the same network.

   - **Follow App Instructions**: The Leica FOTOS app facilitates this process, guiding you through the setup for wireless transfers.

Considerations

- **Transfer Speed**: Transferring larger files, such as RAW DNG images or 4K video, may take longer, especially over wireless connections. It is recommended to batch transfer files to save time.

- **File Formats**: The D-Lux 8 allows you to save images in both JPEG and RAW (DNG) formats, providing flexibility for editing and storage.

- **Battery Life**: Ensure that the camera has sufficient battery life before initiating transfers, especially if using wireless methods.

By utilizing these methods, you can effectively transfer your photos from the Leica D-Lux 8 to your computer for editing, storage, or sharing.

CHAPTER ELEVEN
ACCESSORIES AND COMPATIBILITY

Compatible Lenses and Accessories

The Leica D-Lux 8 is compatible with a range of accessories and utilizes a specific lens designed for its compact format. Here's an overview of the compatible lenses and accessories for the D-Lux 8:

Compatible Lens

- **Leica DC Vario-Summilux 10.9–34mm f/1.7–2.8 ASPH**:
    - This is the built-in zoom lens of the D-Lux 8, providing a 35mm equivalent focal length of **24-75mm**. It features a fast aperture range of **f/1.7 to f/2.8**, making it suitable for various lighting conditions and allowing for creative depth-of-field effects.

Accessories

1. **Flash Unit**:
    - The D-Lux 8 comes with an included Leica CF D flash unit, which can be attached via the accessory shoe. This compact flash enhances low-light photography and helps reduce shadows in portrait shots.

2. **Filters**:
    - The lens has a filter thread size of E43, allowing for the attachment of various filters, including polarizers and ND filters, to enhance image quality and achieve specific effects.

3. **Tripods and Mounts**:
    - The D-Lux 8 features a standard 1/4"-20 tripod thread, allowing it to be mounted on various tripods and stabilizers for steady shooting.

4. **Camera Bag**:
    - While not a specific accessory, using a padded camera bag designed for compact cameras can help protect the D-Lux 8 during transport.

5. **Extra Batteries**:
    - Given the average battery life, carrying extra Leica BP-DC15 batteries is advisable for extended shooting sessions.

6. **Memory Cards**:
    - The D-Lux 8 supports UHS-I and UHS-II SD/SDHC/SDXC memory cards, allowing for fast read/write speeds, especially important for high-resolution image and 4K video recording.

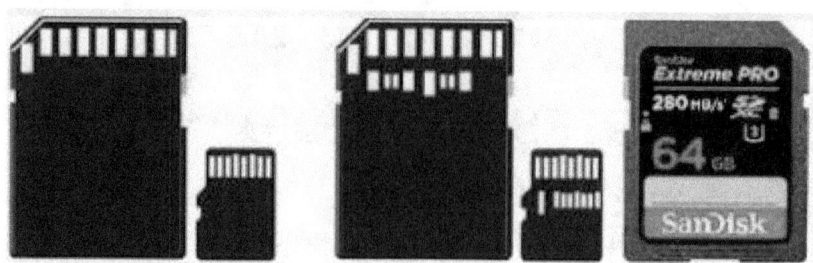

7. **Leica FOTOS App**:
    - The camera features built-in **Wi-Fi** and **Bluetooth**, enabling connectivity with the **Leica FOTOS app** for easy photo transfer, remote shooting, and camera control from a smartphone or tablet.

8. **Lens Cap**:
    - The D-Lux 8 includes a **lens cap** to protect the lens when not in use, preventing dust and scratches.

These lenses and accessories enhance the versatility and functionality of the Leica D-Lux 8, making it suitable for a wide range of photography styles and conditions.

Using Tripods and Other Supports

Using tripods and other supports can significantly enhance your photography, especially in scenarios that require stability and precision. Here's a concise overview of how to effectively use tripods and alternative supports with your camera, including the **Leica D-Lux 8**.

Benefits of Using a Tripod

1. **Stability**: Tripods eliminate camera shake, allowing for sharper images, especially in low-light conditions or when using slow shutter speeds. This is crucial for landscape photography, long exposures, and HDR imaging where precision is essential.

2. **Long Exposures**: A tripod allows you to use longer exposure times without introducing blur. This is particularly useful for capturing smooth water effects, star trails, or any scene requiring a prolonged exposure.

3. **Depth of Field Control**: Using a tripod enables you to shoot at smaller apertures (higher f-stop numbers) for greater depth of field without worrying about camera shake, thus improving the overall sharpness of the image.

4. **Compositional Precision**: With a tripod, you can frame your shots more carefully. It allows for easy adjustments in composition without losing your setup, making it easier to experiment with different angles and perspectives.

5. **Special Techniques**: Tripods are essential for techniques like panoramas, time-lapse photography, and macro photography, where stability is critical for capturing multiple frames or intricate details.

When to Use a Tripod

- **Low Light Conditions**: When shooting in dim lighting, a tripod is almost necessary to avoid motion blur.

- **Slow Shutter Speeds**: If your shutter speed is slower than the reciprocal of your focal length (e.g., 1/200s for a 200mm lens), a tripod is recommended to prevent blur.

- **Macro Photography**: Close-up shots often require precise focus and stability, making a tripod invaluable.

- **HDR and Panoramic Shots**: For HDR photography, where multiple exposures are combined, a stable platform is crucial to avoid misalignment. Similarly, a tripod helps maintain consistent framing in panoramic shots.

Alternatives to Traditional Tripods

If a tripod is not available, you can use various supports:

- **Surrounding Objects**: Use stable surfaces like rocks, walls, or tables to rest your camera. Ensure it's secure to avoid falls.

- **Beanbags**: These can provide a stable platform on uneven surfaces and are portable.

- **Mini Tripods**: Compact and lightweight, these can be useful for quick setups or when space is limited.

- **Camera Straps**: Tying the camera strap around a stable object can provide additional support when shooting.

Tips for Using a Tripod Effectively

1. **Setup**: Ensure all legs are firmly locked and spread wide for maximum stability. Avoid extending the centre column unless necessary, as it can introduce wobble.

2. **Weight Distribution**: Hang a camera bag or weight from the centre column to add stability, especially in windy conditions.

3. **Use a Remote or Timer**: To avoid camera shake when pressing the shutter, use a remote release or the camera's self-timer.

4. **Check Composition**: Once set up, take your time to adjust the composition without rushing. A tripod allows for careful framing.

5. **Consider the Environment**: Set up on stable surfaces and avoid soft ground which can lead to sinking or instability.

In summary, using a tripod or alternative supports can greatly enhance your photography by providing stability, allowing for longer exposures, and enabling more precise compositions. Whether you're shooting landscapes, portraits, or macro images, incorporating a tripod into your workflow can lead to sharper, more professional-quality photos.

Optional External Microphones

The Leica D-Lux (Typ 109) does not have a dedicated microphone input, so it does not natively support external microphones directly. However, if you need improved audio quality for video recording, here are some alternative approaches you can consider:

1. Using an External Recorder

- **Description:** Use a separate audio recording device (e.g., a portable audio recorder) to capture high-quality audio while recording video with the Leica D-Lux (Typ 109).

- **How to Use:**

  - **Record Audio Separately:** Set up the external microphone with the audio recorder to capture the desired sound.

  - **Synchronize Audio and Video:** After recording, sync the audio from the external recorder with the video footage during the editing process using video editing software.

2. Bluetooth Microphones

- **Description:** Some Bluetooth microphones can record audio wirelessly and might offer better quality than the built-in microphone.

- **How to Use:**

  - **Pair with Recording Device:** Connect the Bluetooth microphone to a compatible recording device or app.

  - **Record and Sync:** Similar to using an external recorder, record audio separately and sync it with your video during post-production.

3. Smartphone or Tablet Integration

- **Description:** Use your smartphone or tablet as an external audio recorder. Some apps can use your device's microphone or connect to external microphones for better audio quality.

- **How to Use:**

  - **Select an App:** Choose an audio recording app that allows high-quality audio capture.

  - **Record Separately:** Record the audio using the app while you capture video with the Leica D-Lux (Typ 109).

  - **Sync in Post-Production:** Synchronize the audio and video during editing.

4. Clip-On Microphones (Lavalier Mics)

- **Description:** Lavalier microphones can be used with a separate recording device to capture clear audio. These are useful for interviews or situations where the subject is close to the microphone.

- **How to Use:**
  - **Connect to External Recorder:** Attach the lavalier microphone to an external audio recorder.
  - **Record and Sync:** Record audio separately and synchronize with video in post-production.

5. Audio Quality Tips

- **Positioning:** Place the external microphone close to the sound source to capture clear audio.
- **Windshields:** Use windshields or windjammers for outdoor recording to reduce wind noise.
- **Monitoring:** Use headphones to monitor audio quality during recording.

While the **Leica D-Lux (Typ 109)** does not support external microphones directly, you can still achieve high-quality audio by using separate recording devices or smartphones with external microphones. After recording, you will need to synchronize the audio with your video footage in post-production for the best results.

CHAPTER TWELVE
MAINTEMNANCE AND CARE

Cleaning the Camera and Lens

Cleaning your **Leica D-Lux 8** camera and lens is essential for maintaining image quality and ensuring the longevity of your equipment. Here's a comprehensive guide on how to clean both effectively:

Cleaning the Camera Body

1. **Gather Your Tools**:
   - **Lens blower**: To remove dust and debris without touching the surface.
   - **Soft-bristled brush**: For gently brushing away particles.
   - **Microfiber cloth**: For wiping the camera body.
   - **Lens cleaning solution**: Specifically formulated for camera lenses (avoid household cleaners).

2. **Power Off the Camera**: Always turn off your camera before cleaning to prevent accidental damage.

3. **Remove the Lens**: If applicable, detach the lens from the camera body to clean both components separately.

4. **Dust Removal**:
   - Use the lens blower to remove loose dust from the camera body and lens.
   - Follow up with a soft-bristled brush to gently sweep away any remaining particles.

5. **Wipe the Body**:
   - Use a clean microfiber cloth to wipe the camera body gently. Avoid using excessive force, especially around buttons and dials.

6. **Inspect for Residue**: Check for any stubborn smudges or dirt. If necessary, lightly dampen a corner of the microfiber cloth with lens cleaning solution and carefully wipe the affected areas.

Cleaning the Lens

1. **Prepare for Lens Cleaning**:
   - Ensure you have a lens cleaning kit that includes lens tissue or wipes, a blower, and a cleaning solution.

2. **Initial Dust Removal**:
   - Start by using the lens blower to remove any loose dust or debris from the lens surface. Hold the blower a few inches away from the lens.

3. **Brush Away Particles**:
   - If there's stubborn dust remaining, use a soft-bristled lens brush to gently remove it.

4. **Apply Cleaning Solution**:
   - Dab a small amount of lens cleaning solution onto a clean lens tissue or microfiber cloth. Avoid applying the solution directly to the lens.

5. **Clean the Lens Surface**:
   - Using a circular motion, start cleaning from the center of the lens and move outward toward the edges. This technique helps prevent pushing dirt towards the center.

6. **Inspect for Streaks**: After cleaning, check the lens for any streaks or smudges. If needed, use a dry part of the cloth to buff out any remaining marks.

7. **Use a Lens Cleaning Pen (Optional)**:
   - If you have a lens cleaning pen, use the brush end to remove any remaining particles and the cleaning tip for a thorough clean.

Additional Tips

- **Avoid Compressed Air**: Do not use compressed air, as it can introduce moisture or propel dirt into the lens assembly.
- **Keep Lens Caps On**: Always attach the lens cap when the camera is not in use to prevent dust accumulation.
- **Store Properly**: Store your camera in a dry, dust-free environment and use a camera bag for added protection.
- **Regular Maintenance**: Clean your camera and lens regularly, especially if you frequently shoot in dusty or humid conditions.

By following these steps, you can keep your Leica D-Lux 8 clean and in optimal working condition, ensuring that it continues to deliver high-quality images.

Storing the Camera

Proper storage of your **Leica D-Lux 8** camera is essential to maintain its performance and longevity. Here are detailed guidelines on how to effectively store your camera and its accessories:

Preparing for Storage

1. **Clean Your Gear**: Before storing your camera, ensure it is clean. Wipe down the camera body and lens with a microfiber cloth to remove dust, fingerprints, and smudges. This prevents dirt from settling and causing damage over time.

2. **Remove Batteries and Memory Cards**: If you don't plan to use the camera for an extended period, remove the battery and memory card. This helps prevent battery leakage and ensures that the memory card does not get stuck in the camera.

3. **Use Lens and Screen Protectors**: Attach lens caps and screen protectors to safeguard against scratches and dust accumulation while in storage.

Choosing the Right Storage Environment

1. **Cool and Dry Location**: Store your camera in a cool, dry place away from direct sunlight and heat sources. Avoid areas prone to humidity, such as basements or attics, as moisture can lead to Mold and corrosion.

2. **Humidity Control**: Consider using silica gel packets or a dehumidifier in your storage area to absorb excess moisture. This is especially important if you live in a humid climate.

3. **Airtight Containers**: For long-term storage, consider placing your camera and lenses in airtight containers. This helps keep out moisture and dust, providing an extra layer of protection.

Storage Solutions

1. **Camera Bags and Cases**: Use padded camera bags or hard cases for protection. These bags often come with compartments to keep your camera, lenses, and accessories organized and cushioned against impacts.

2. **Shelving and Cubbies**: Modular shelves or cubbies can be effective for organizing your gear. Assign specific areas for different items, such as lenses, batteries, and memory cards, to keep everything easily accessible.

3. **Dry Cabinets**: Invest in a dry cabinet specifically designed for camera gear. These cabinets maintain low humidity levels, creating an ideal environment for your camera and lenses.

4. **Avoiding Tangling**: Use hooks or pegboards to hang camera straps and cords, preventing them from becoming tangled and damaged.

Regular Maintenance

- **Check Your Gear**: Periodically inspect your stored camera and accessories for any signs of moisture or damage. This allows you to address any issues before they worsen.

- **Replace Silica Gel**: If using silica gel packets, replace them regularly to ensure they remain effective in absorbing moisture.

By following these guidelines, you can ensure that your Leica D-Lux 8 and its accessories remain in excellent condition, ready for your next photography adventure. Proper storage not only protects your investment but also enhances your overall shooting experience.

Updating Firmware

Updating the firmware on the Leica D-Lux 8 is an important process to ensure your camera operates with the latest features, improvements, and bug fixes. Here's a step-by-step guide on how to update the firmware:

Steps to Update Firmware

1. **Check Current Firmware Version**:
   - Power on your camera.
   - Go to the **Menu** and navigate to the **Settings** section.
   - Select **Firmware Version** to view the current version installed on your camera.

2. **Download the Latest Firmware**:
   - Visit the official Leica website and navigate to the **D-Lux 8** product page.
   - Look for the **Support** or **Downloads** section where firmware updates are listed.
   - Download the latest firmware file to your computer. Ensure that you download the correct version for your specific camera model.

3. **Prepare the Memory Card**:
   - Insert a compatible memory card into your computer.
   - Format the memory card in the camera to ensure it is clean and ready for the firmware update. This can typically be done in the **Menu** under **Settings > Format Card**.

4. **Transfer Firmware to Memory Card**:
   - Copy the downloaded firmware file onto the root directory of the memory card (do not place it in any folders).

5. **Insert the Memory Card into the Camera**:
   - Safely eject the memory card from your computer and insert it back into the camera.

6. **Start the Firmware Update**:
   - Power on the camera.
   - Go to the **Menu** and navigate to the **Settings** section again.

- Select **Firmware Update**.
- The camera will detect the new firmware file on the memory card. Follow the on-screen instructions to begin the update process.

7. **Complete the Update**:
   - Do not turn off the camera or remove the memory card during the update process, as this can cause damage to the camera's firmware.
   - Once the update is complete, the camera will usually restart automatically.

8. **Verify the Update**:
   - After the camera restarts, check the firmware version again to ensure that the update was successful.

Additional Notes

- **Battery Charge**: Ensure that your camera's battery is fully charged before starting the update to avoid any interruptions.
- **Read the Release Notes**: Before updating, it's a good idea to read the release notes provided with the firmware update. This will inform you of any new features, improvements, or fixes included in the update.
- **Open Source Code**: The D-Lux 8 is noted to be an open-source camera, with its source code available for download. However, the firmware updates provided by Leica are proprietary and should be followed as per the official instructions to avoid any issues.

By following these steps, you can successfully update the firmware on your Leica D-Lux 8, ensuring optimal performance and access to the latest features.

Troubleshooting Common Issues

Here are some common issues you may encounter with the Leica D-Lux 8 and how to troubleshoot them:

Camera Won't Turn On

- **Check that the battery is properly inserted and charged**. Make sure the battery contacts are clean and undamaged.
- **If using an external charger, ensure it is compatible and functioning properly**. Try charging the battery in the camera using the USB-C port.
- **If the camera still doesn't power on, contact Leica support for further assistance**.

Blurry or Out-of-Focus Images

- **Check that the lens is clean and free of smudges or scratches**. Clean the lens carefully using a microfiber cloth.

- **Ensure the camera is not in macro mode when trying to focus on distant subjects.** Switch to normal autofocus mode.
- **Make sure the subject is within the camera's focus range.** The D-Lux 8 can focus as close as 3cm at wide-angle.
- **If autofocus is consistently missing, try calibrating the lens or contact Leica support.**

Memory Card Issues

- **Ensure the memory card is properly formatted in the camera.** Avoid formatting on a computer.
- **Check that the card is compatible with the camera's specifications.** Use a high-speed UHS-I or UHS-II SDHC/SDXC card.
- **If the camera doesn't recognize the card, try reformatting it in the camera. If issues persist, the card may be damaged and should be replaced.**

Overheating and Shutdown

- **The D-Lux 8 may overheat during extended 4K video recording or in hot environments.** Allow the camera to cool down before resuming use.
- **Avoid leaving the camera in direct sunlight for prolonged periods when not in use.**
- **If overheating occurs frequently, contact Leica support as it may indicate a hardware issue.**

Connectivity Problems

- **Ensure the camera's firmware is up-to-date.** Check for and install any available firmware updates.
- **Make sure Bluetooth and Wi-Fi are enabled in the camera settings.** Pair the camera with the Leica Fotos app.
- **If wireless connectivity is unreliable, move the camera closer to the connected device or router.**
- **If issues persist, reset the camera's network settings in the menu.**

For any other issues or if problems continue after troubleshooting, contact Leica's customer support for further assistance. They can provide more specific guidance or arrange for the camera to be serviced if needed.

CHAPTER THIRTEEN
TECHNICAL SPECIFICATION

Camera Specifications

The Leica D-Lux 8 is a compact digital camera that combines advanced features with a user-friendly design. Here are the key specifications:

- **Camera Type**: Digital compact camera

- **Dimensions**: 130 x 69 x 62 mm (5.1 x 2.7 x 2.4 inches)

- **Weight**: Approx. 397 g (14 ounces) with battery; 357 g without battery

- **Sensor**:

    - Type: 4/3" CMOS sensor

    - Total Megapixels: 21.77 MP

    - Effective Megapixels: 17 MP

- **Lens**:

    - Model: Leica DC Vario-Summilux 10.9–34mm f/1.7–2.8 ASPH

    - 35mm Equivalent: 24–75mm

    - Aperture Range: f/1.7 to f/16 (wide), f/2.8 to f/16 (tele)

- **Image Stabilization**: Visual compensation system for photos and video recordings

- **ISO Sensitivity**: ISO 100 to 25,600

- **Image Formats**:

    - Photo: DNG (raw), DNG + JPEG, JPEG

    - Video: MP4, H.264, AAC stereo

- **Video Recording**: 4K video capability

- **Storage Medium**: UHS-II (recommended), UHS-I, SD/SDHC/SDXC memory cards

- **Viewfinder**: 2.36-million dot OLED electronic viewfinder

- **LCD Screen**: 3-inch TFT LCD with approximately 1,843,200 dots

- **Battery**:

    - Type: Lithium-ion (Leica BP-DC15)

    - Approximate Shots: 240 (using EVF), 300 (using LCD)

- **Connectivity**:

    - USB 3.1 Gen 1 Type C (for charging and data transfer)

- HDMI Type D output
- ISO accessory shoe for external flash units
- **Operating Conditions**: 0°C to +40°C
- **File Formats**: Supports DNG, JPEG, and video formats like MP4.
- **Tripod Thread**: 1/4 DIN 4503 (1/4")
- **Flash**: Includes a compact attachable flash unit.
- **Customizable Controls**: Features a command dial that can be customized for various functions.

These specifications highlight the Leica D-Lux 8's capabilities as a versatile and compact camera, suitable for both casual and more serious photography. Its combination of a high-quality lens, advanced sensor, and compact design makes it a popular choice among photographers seeking portability without sacrificing image quality.

Lens Specifications

The Leica D-Lux 8 is equipped with a high-quality lens that enhances its photographic capabilities. Here are the detailed specifications of the lens:

- **Model**: Leica DC Vario-Summilux 10.9–34mm f/1.7–2.8 ASPH
- **Focal Length**:
    - 10.9–34mm (equivalent to 24–75mm in 35mm full-frame terms)
- **Aperture Range**:
    - Maximum aperture of f/1.7 at the wide end (10.9mm) and f/2.8 at the telephoto end (34mm).
    - Minimum aperture of f/16 across both focal lengths.
- **Optical Construction**:
    - The lens includes aspherical elements to minimize optical aberrations and enhance image quality.
- **Focus Modes**:
    - The lens features a manual focus, autofocus, and macro autofocus switch, allowing for versatile focusing options.
- **Close Focus Distance**:
    - Minimum focus distance of 3cm (1.2 inches) in macro mode, enabling detailed close-up photography.
- **Filter Thread**:

- The lens has a filter thread size of E43, allowing the attachment of various filters.

- **Image Stabilization**:
    - The lens incorporates a visual compensation system to help reduce camera shake, particularly useful during handheld shooting.

- **Aspect Ratio Slider**:
    - An aspect ratio slider located on the lens allows for quick adjustments between different image formats.

- **Manual Focus Ring**:
    - The lens features a dedicated manual focus ring, which can be adjusted for either linear or non-linear focus control.

- **Detent Aperture Ring**:
    - The aperture ring allows for smooth adjustments in 1/3-stop increments, providing precise control over exposure settings.

These specifications highlight the versatility and quality of the Leica D-Lux 8's lens, making it suitable for a wide range of photographic situations, from landscapes to portraits and macro photography. The combination of a fast aperture and a flexible zoom range contributes to its performance in various lighting conditions.

Battery Life and Usage

The Leica D-Lux 8 features a lithium-ion battery (Leica BP-DC15) with a rated capacity of 1025 mAh and a voltage of 7.2V. Here are the key points regarding battery life and usage:

Battery Life

- **CIPA Ratings**: The camera is rated for approximately **240 shots** when using the electronic viewfinder (EVF) and **300 shots** with the LCD screen under standard testing conditions. However, real-world performance may vary.

- **User Experiences**: Some users report that the battery life can be less than expected, with experiences indicating that the battery level may drop significantly after a short period of use. It is suggested that users may need to rely on extra batteries for extended shooting sessions, especially during intensive use.

- **Charging**: The D-Lux 8 supports in-camera charging via a **USB-C** connection. This allows for convenient charging while on the go, although the USB-C port is primarily for power and not for data transfer.

- **Third-Party Options**: The battery used in the D-Lux 8 is compatible with other models, such as the Panasonic LX100, making it easier to find third-party replacements or additional batteries.

Usage Tips

- **Carry Extra Batteries**: Given the average battery life, it is advisable to carry at least one extra battery, especially for longer outings or events.

- **Use Power Banks**: Since the camera can charge via USB-C, using a power bank can be an effective way to recharge the battery while on the move.

- **Monitor Battery Levels**: Keep an eye on the battery level indicator, as it can sometimes show a promising charge before dropping quickly.

In summary, while the Leica D-Lux 8 offers decent battery performance, users should be prepared for the possibility of needing additional batteries for extended use, especially during intensive shooting sessions.

THANK YOU FOR READING